# BROWN PAPER SUGA: ROUND 2

By: Cheraee C.

C'Cliche
The Queen Pen

Brown Paper Sugar: Round 2

ISBN: 978-1-513648-76-7


Published by C'Cliché LLC
Email: sosyree@gmail.com

## Acknowledgements

C'Cliché thanks, appreciates, and congratulates all the amazing authors and poets who made it to another round of Brown Paper Suga. This is the second edition to the Brown Paper Suga Series where C'Cliché helps authors gain exposure and publication. Being featured in this compilation project is just the beginning for all of these authors who will all began their independent and individual journeys to birthing a book. So in the wise words of Nipsey Hussle, "the real marathon continues."

Louise (A.L.) Brown

Sherri (Sasha) Brown

Giovanni Bowers

Kiara (Rashai) Williams

Jordan (J.Focuz) Harris

Don McCaskill

Shamika (Ice) Bowers

Sable Johnson

## Table of Contents

### Stories



### Poetry

## ***The Copier***

Author: A. L. Brown

I am put together piece by piece, highly technical, and require a certain expertise to assemble me. I am multifunctional, able to sort, stack, staple, and have several storage drawers. I guess you wonder what I am. I am the copier on the third floor of the Welcome Center at Wayne State University. My jobs can be large or small depending on your demand. I mostly sit alone in the corner on the energy's saving mode. I smile and light up when my top is open. Sometimes my system gets thrown off because some of you don't take time to get to know me and understand how I function. I'd rather go back to the warehouse than listen to you all talk about how obese someone is or what someone is wearing. I wish I could ask every one of you if you looked in the mirror lately. Some of you people should stay out of office politics and focus on self-improvement and not self-destruction. The truth of the matter is, you treat me as if I caused the dilemma in your life. I am tired of you pushing the wrong buttons and screwing up my settings. I was treated much better in the warehouse. You people make me feel so unhappy at times that I'd rather be shipped somewhere more pleasant where people are friendlier. I get tired of you slamming my top down, it's not my fault you missed the in-service on how I operate. Get it together or I will shut down every time you come to me with some work.

I have somewhat recuperated from the shock you sent me through when my top was slammed. I'm glad you decided to move out of the way so, that the office snitches can use me. The office snitches are wannabe's with the Head of the Department. The office snitches are always hanging around me with their sneaky, backstabbing ways talking bout everyone in the office. They smile in your face and stab you in the back kinda people. They are the office's biggest gossip bugs, I hear the saying "girl guess what I heard, she is so ghetto and have the nerve to think that she has class." This is another group I'm tired of listening to. The last thing they want to do is to identify who this person is and they are careful not to mention names around here. A person could get into big trouble spreading gossip and causing the only copier on the third floor to malfunction. I guess they don't trust me to keep a secret. People do come around me all the time sharing good and bad news, it's not always gossip. Some people don't care about what the office says or thinks. If they only could hear how I feel about gossip bugs. I wished I could say to them, "have you thought just maybe that they don't give a damn about what you people have to say about them while you are standing here in front of me marking copies." There's one thing for sure, you haven't yet mastered me even though you spend time around me to know how I function. You change my size, you even fumble with my tone from light to dark. Strangely, you see well enough to notice moles and pimples on another person's face but, you can't get my functions right. Seems to me you would keep me on dark mode, since those new prescription designer glasses you have are not strong enough. I pause and jam up purposely while they try to figure out how to get me back going again, I can hear some more gossip. People that gossip are miserable and want to make other people feel the same way they feel. Gossip always keeps confusion and discord among employees and it sets the tone for a very unhealthy work environment. Standing in front of me pissed off is not the solution to the problem. You can't find the man you are looking for in this corner. There's nothing over here, but me and different size papers, and a waste paper basket for the bad copies. After all, you spend more time complaining about other people and not enough time trying to learn how I function. Maybe I'll shut down again and give you all a reality check. Open my top and lean over so I can see how you look. Have you noticed I shut down for ten minutes and you still haven't figured out the problem with me? Figuring out how to get me up and operating again should be relatively easy since you have time to pry into other employees lives. If I could communicate other than breaking down I would ask, "why are you being so judgmental towards people you don't know?" You spend so much time around me and I remain a mystery to some of you. It's time to hit reset and go to the next job.

My next job should be smooth and simple because here comes my friend who was trained how to use me, I call her the “Copy Queen." She's friendly and always has kind words to say about people regardless of who they are and where they come from. She always loads the paper from the top and switches me on automatic feed. While on automatic feed there's no need to stand around and wait for me to stop because I'll complete the job and have it waiting for pick-up. There's a slim chance that I will hear some more juicy office gossip when I'm on automatic feed because I'm too busy, so they will go stand around somewhere else. I have five more minutes and I'm finished with this job. There was so much paper shooting out and my compartments were moving so fast that I couldn't count fast enough. Finally, I am at the end of this job and now I'm in the cool down mode. I'm just waiting for the “Copy Queen” to pick up this job. It's getting towards the end of the day and I'm waiting on the next person to use me while my compartments are still cooling down. Lately, there's been a lot of talk about misusing me and wasting paper around here. I am not surprised with all that extra paper in the waste paper basket and the paper that gets stuck inside of me. The Big Officials’ documents are tossed into the waste paper basket without being properly disposed. There's no telling where the information may turn up. The worst case scenario is that the envious and hateful employees find them and use the information fraudulently.

My best time is when I'm performing jobs for staff from the fourth floor. It's usually, information for a number of open house events and the flyers for new student information packages. These jobs contain lots of details, graphics, and colors. As a matter of fact, the entire jobs are filled with bright colors. When I do jobs of this nature I get a chance to see where the Big Officials are hanging out and what kind of refreshments will be served. Most of the students get curious and may sneak up the stairs or the elevator to the third floor, so that they can toy with my buttons. I realize that the students aren't trying to harm me like the regular staff. The students just want to make copies of their homework and copy nasty pictures and posters. It's apparent that the students are more knowledgeable about my functions than the majority of staff members working in this department. They can come back to use me anytime, I will gladly welcome them.

Don't misunderstand me, there are a few hard working good people in this department. These people are respectful and polite to staff and they also, stay away from office politics and office cliques. I'm just the copier sitting in the corner all day and I only deal with people that come around me. If I could decide where I would be sitting, I would choose the fourth floor. Creativity takes place on that floor. For example, invitations for office parties, anniversaries, bridal showers, and birthday parties are always circulating on the fourth floor. There's always the smell of food present. Someone is always eating something that smells up the whole floor. If I got the chance to be on the fourth floor who knows I may get a chance to see the President Dr. Reed and Susan walk through the office. Things get quiet when they come to the floor.

Confessions Of A
Golddigger
By Giovanni B

Getting what I want has always been a hobby of mine and by any means necessary has always been my motto. My name is Ava Porter and I'm an aspiring actress out of Detroit which is a place so far from Hollywood people don't even dream as big as I do.

My looks have gotten me far in life. I realized that early on around 12 or 13 to be exact. I was born to a black single mother and a white Italian father that I never met. By the time I was 16, men started to notice how I looked which isn't much different than now. I'm 5'4, have naturally long hair, light skinned, dimples, hazel eyes, with a face as pretty as Aaliyah and Lauren London, and a body like Teyana Taylor. My looks helped me learn how to utilize men who would sell their soul just to have a woman like me on their arm. My love of money came from the lack of it that I had growing up. My mother made the best of what she had, but it helped me to want more. I didn't see myself getting more by working these half-assed paying 9-5's needing two of them just to get by.

Growing up I loved Lil' Kim, she empowered me. I never heard a woman talk like her, and she gave me my motto, "why spend mine, when I can spend yours." I could spot a man that was worth my while a mile away and my radar has only gotten better with time.

My first serious boyfriend was CJ. He looked like Sticky Fingaz from the rap group Onyx and the movie Ride back in his prime in the 90's. He was 23 and I was 17. He was gangsta, but he was always nice to me. He always smelled like expensive cologne and good weed, and I knew he sold dope, but I minded my business and stayed in his pockets. CJ drove a 2002 brand new all black Cadillac Escalade. I remember him dropping me off to school every morning my whole senior year. I was the only chick in school wearing a jewelry set from Tiffany's with the bracelet and the necklace. So many hoes were jealous of me, but none of them would dream of touching me because they knew CJ's name held weight all over the westside of Detroit. After CJ took my virginity he decided he didn't want another nigga touching me ever, and I decided I wanted to move into his riverfront apartment downtown. At that point I was almost 18 so my momma had already lost her grip on me. Plus CJ was helping pay her bills too per my request.

My goal in life was never to be a drug dealer's wife or even a girlfriend too long. CJ loved me and I knew he had other bitches, but I was a kept woman by the time I turned 18. I was driving a 3 series BMW, I didn't have to work, he kept me put up and pretty until it was time to hit the city and he wanted to show me off, or when we went on our every 3 month vacations. By the end of 2003, I admit I was loving my life, but I was bored. There wasn't many auditions coming to Detroit and after I graduated from DSA (a performing arts school in Detroit) I wasn't even working on my craft anymore.

My bestfriend at the time was CJ's boy Fat Mike's girl Angel. Angel was a dancer, she was brown-skinned, beautiful, and stacked. Her body was what the girls now pay for, and the only thing she paid for was the titties. Angel had jumped on to the wave of doing music videos. She had done a few for a lot of big artists at that time. Her girls in Atlanta hooked her up with gigs. It was just what fly chicks did in that era. As for me, I wanted to be a serious actress like Jada Pinkett or Sanaa Lathan. I didn't see myself shaking my ass in videos, and I knew CJ wasn't going for that. When I discovered that the girls were making 4-5k or more per video at that time, it slightly caught my interest, and I looked at it as a chance to be on TV. I knew I couldn't be honest about why I was flying out to Atlanta because CJ would flip the fuck out, so me and Angel just said were taking a girls' trip and was doing some shopping, CJ was looking at that as an opportunity to cheat all weekend and not have me questioning shit so he gave me 7 g's and sent me on my way. Little did he or I know what Atlanta had in store for me.

Arriving in Atlanta, meeting Angel's girls, and all the vixens I had seen in some of my favorite videos, I was amazed. It was the first time I had ever been intimidated around other females even though they all told me how pretty I was. Our very first night we were at a party with Pimp C, Bun B, and Three 6 Mafia. I watched all the girls flock to the rappers while I sat back in the cut with a drink. I was coming out here to maybe be in the background of a video or two. In my mind I had a man that was a good catch. By the time 2am came, I assumed we were going back to the hotel room. I was good and tired, we left in a limo, and pulled up to this big house, probably the nicest house I ever seen in person. When we pulled in the gates, I saw the big trucks and video crews, and Angel whispered in my ear, "you ready new booty?" I was in shock like damn it's after 2am and we shooting a video. I'm not even ready, but then as we were dropped off by this big trailer in the back of the house, we were let out and escorted into hair and makeup. Some of the girls I saw in the club and Angel's friends were here. We got quick hair and makeup touchups and there were racks and racks of swimsuits for us to put on. My information was taken by a woman who said she would make sure she got us paid. Half naked and uncomfortable, I followed all the other girls up to the house where filming had started. As the shoot went on about an hour in, I got more comfortable when the camera started rolling. It was like I was a natural so much so that Pimp C moved me to the front next to Angel and Melyssa Ford, and we got a lot more camera shots than the other girls. When it was time to go we were given checks. I had made 5k in one night and I got to feel like a star. I could get used to this.

That weekend I shot over three music videos, made 15k, and was moved to one of the main girls in all three of them. I was excited to see myself on TV, but I was not ready to go home and tell CJ what I did on my girls' trip, but I didn't care. I knew I belonged in front of a camera. Something about me had changed. I finally felt like I arrived. My attitude changed and I was feeling like that bitch after one weekend. I remember depositing my money in the bank, opening up my own account for the first time, with money I said I wouldn't touch as long as I didn't need to. By the time CJ found out I was doing videos I had already flew out to LA with Angel and had done two more. He flipped his shit, but I told him I wasn't willing to stop, and that made things between us rocky, and he started to question me more. By the start of 2004, I had a nice little savings of my own. CJ was staying out all night and not caring what I had to say about it. I could tell our situation was running its course, but shit

I never lived alone, and he still didn't want to see me with anyone else.

Angel called me up and told me that someone had been sweating her about meeting me. He had seen me in a few videos and no one had my info. Naturally I was curious, even though at this point I was still loyal to CJ. My phone rang one day and I heard a deep voice on the other end, one that was familiar with a heavy New York accent. Even once I figured out who it was, I played dumb.

"Who is this?"

He replied, "this E Rock, what’s up with you ma?" He told me he was a fan of mine like he wasn't one of the biggest rappers out. He asked if he could fly me out for a video of his all expenses covered, which naturally caught my ear. E had only given me two days to pack and I didn't even explain to CJ where I was going, I would usually fuck him real good before I left, but fucking him was the last thing on my mind. I hopped on my paid for first class flight to New York and loved every minute of it. I assumed I would only be in New York for a day or so and the video shoot would be the same or next day, but when I got there E picked me up from the airport in a clean white Range Rover just him and his security guard Tay. He asked me if I was hungry, next thing you know we were at Mr. Chows. I pretended not to be too impressed even though I knew that’s where all the celebrities went and ate. People came up to him and greeted him, but he still made me feel like I was the VIP.

After lunch he took me on a shopping spree Gucci, Louis Vuitton, Neiman Marcus, and I didn't have to spend a dime. A part of me felt guilty, but then again who was I to turn down a shopping spree. On the ride to the hotel, I asked him about the video shoot. He admitted that he lied about the shoot to get me down here, and I told him right then and there that I have a man. He still insisted that I let him show me a beautiful few days with no strings attached, and I almost declined until he offered to take me as his escort to the Vibe Awards, and that I could not turn down. I loved E's music, but I never paid attention to how fine he was. He was tall, 6'4, brown-skinned, full lips, and a gym made body. I never met a rapper that looked like Tyson Beckford, but was still a G to his core. E dropped me off at the hotel. He told me he would be back in a couple hours to come take me to dinner, and that he had to run to the studio. The door man came and helped me with my tons of shopping bags and suitcases, and led me in. I checked in and got my room key where I was led to the 13th floor where the presidential suites were. I had never been in a hotel this nice let along a presidential suite. It made all my trips with CJ look small time and I wanted the big time. I took a hot bubble bath and slipped into one of the beautiful outfits I brought that day. I didn't wanna under dress or overdress.

I realized I didn't call "My Man" all day, but I called Angel to tell her about how my trip started. She wanted all the details and I spilled a few, and I never told her it was no video shoot. That night we had dinner on E's yacht. We had a three course meal and he never talked about his career. He listened to me talk about my goals of being an actress and actually offered to introduce me to some of the right people. He looked me in the eye the whole conversation and it turned me on to hear him offer to invest in me. As the evening winded down and it got dark, E invited me out on the deck to look at the stars and how pretty the water looked at night. Caught up in the moment I let him kiss me and I know for a fact I kissed back. He smelled so good and his hands felt so good over my body, but I pushed him away reminding him that I had a man. I could tell he was a little irritated because he swallowed down his glass of champagne and asked me was I ready to bounce. I figured it was time so we went back to the limo and I was dropped back off at the hotel. I called and talked to CJ that night for about 20 minutes. He acted like he was too busy to talk so I took a bath and laid in that big king sized bed and I got mine. I have never played with my pussy more intensely than I did this night and all I could think about was E. I even called out his government name Erik while I was cumming.

The next day after we went to breakfast, E kept his word and introduced me to a man named Keenan Williams. Keenan was a big time manager to some of the biggest Hollywood stars. He was willing to take a meeting with me even though I had no experience outside of some school plays and my drama classes in high school. Keenan looked at me for a minute before he told E, "man your right she does have the look." He asked me if I had a manager which of course I didn't, and did I have a resume, and headshots. I was reluctant to tell him no, but when I did E told him he can make sure I got all that ASAP. Keenan gave me his card and told me I would be hearing from him as soon as he could get my headshots out there, and told me no more videos.

When we got in the limo, E told me he had a photographer that can hook me up with a headshot and some pics that I can send out. I told him I don't know why he's looking out for me this way. He just explained that he saw potential in me. At this point I was so grateful I kind of threw the pussy at him. I found myself in broad daylight sucking his dick in the back of the limo, while he fingered me before climbing on top of him riding his dick. I was loud. I knew the driver got an earful, but I didn't care. If he had done all this without even getting a taste this should take it to the next level.

I had only ever dreamed about being styled by a stylist with the Vibe Awards being that night, E made that dream come true. He left me with a stylist. She was a French black woman named Celeste who looked like Grace Jones and demanded the room. Her intent was to give me a full makeover. I had gotten the full star treatment. I got a facial, manicure, pedicure, highlights in my hair, eye lashes, she had like 40 dresses and shoes for me to choose from, I felt like a star already. After finding the perfect dress, a black sheer Gucci dress that hugged the curves of my body tight with a low cut front, and a pair of Gucci heels, I had no idea that I would end up matching E when he met me at the hotel.

I felt my heart drop as E and I were pulling up to the Vibe Awards. I was really about to walk a red carpet with a celebrity. I didn't care what my man would think seeing me on TV, all I could think about was the exposure. When I stepped out the limo on the red carpet hand and hand with E, I was instantly addicted to the lights and all the commotion. A reporter for UPN asked, “E-Rock what up with the new album? and who is this beauty on your arm?" He introduced me as a special friend of his who is a model and actress and told them to be on the lookout for me, and that introduction continued to every reporter and photographer. Now for many of you, I'm sure you remember what happened at the 2004 Vibe Awards. That was the infamous night of the big fight that broke out with G-Unit, and I was right there in the middle of everything. It was a night I would never forget. When we got back to the hotel, I was still on a high. That was the first night I ever seen E do cocaine in front of me. We fucked like rabbits especially since I was going back home the next day.

When I got back to Detroit I felt very unsatisfied. I didn't know how to adjust back to reality after I experienced that taste of the celebrity life, and being in LA. Hell I wasn't even sure if E was gonna still try to make stuff happen for me. When my flight landed I knew something was up when CJ didn't pick me up from the airport. He had told my mom to come get me. She told me he told her to take me to breakfast so we could spend some time together. My intuition told me to tell my mom to take me home. I told her I was jetlagged and wanted to rest. When we pulled up to my building I told her to stay in the car. I didn't even grab my luggage out of her trunk. I went up to our floor and I tried to be quiet when I unlocked the door. When I opened the door my intuition never lies… I heard Lil Wayne's new song 'Go Dj' blaring through our speaker system, but that couldn't drown out the moaning of some bitch. Now I was not a fighter, but I was prepared to kick some ass not just his, but hers too. I sat my keys down on the counter, put my hair up in a bun, and burst in the door like a hurricane.

In the bed we shared, this nigga was fucking some slim framed, brown skinned girl. I can honestly say I didn't even get to see her face properly before I snatched her by her weave from off top of him, and whooped her naked ass. I was seeing red and I felt CJ trying to pull me off of her, so I turned around and started swinging on him. The girl grabbed what clothes she could and ran out the apartment with no shoes. I instantly started grabbing my shit out the closet. He grabbed my arm asking, "how you coming in here on that shit when you all on TV like a groupie to that nigga E Rock? You fucking that nigga, bitch?" Naturally I lied and said “no,” but walking away from him was surprisingly easy. I went full on Angela Bassett in 'Waiting to Exhale' and made a grand exit, and it was at that moment I realized that I was incapable of actually loving a man. Being with CJ was beneficial now I had bigger fish to catch. I wasn’t even sad. My mom looked shocked when she seen me coming down with all the shit I could pack between CJ trying to have a fight and stop me from leaving, I told her everything, and I told her that I needed to stay with her for a few days and that I had a plan, and that I truly did have a plan. I called Angel that night and asked her what she thought about moving to LA. I mean I had the money to move, but I didn't wanna move alone. She wasn't really trying to leave her man, she was actually in love as silly as that sounded, so I had to move on to my second plan.

It had been so long since I had my mom’s cooking. It felt good getting that time in with her. I had been paying her bills with the help of CJ, and sending her money, but we hadn’t gotten a lot of quality time. My mom did tell me that she heard I was on TV, and she didn't care to watch me in the videos, but at the awards, she actually seemed proud of me, and that feeling was better than anything. I promised her soon it would be the big screen. Once everything settled that night I called E. I was shocked when he actually answered and I told him everything that happened. He thought the idea of me going crazy like that was funny as hell, and he told me he would fly me back out to LA whenever I was ready so I can get to this money. He even told me that I could stay with him and be his lady. The conversation with E went just as I expected. I knew when I left that the next step was that mansion of his that I had seen on MTV Cribs, but I didn't think it would be this soon, but hey I'm worth it.

By the middle of 2005 I was living with E. We were a couple that people cared about, and people knew my name. I had been in Vibe and Source Magazine by his side. I had done commercials, and I was a featured model for Baby Phat and Von Dutch, I had done some extra roles in TV shows and movies, but still had not had the big break I wanted. E kept his word with making sure I was making moves. It made it easy to ignore his coke habit, and the other women which I knew would come with dating a rapper, but I had a name out here now and a little status. I knew it came with a price. While working as an extra, I made friends with this director Lorenzo Henderson. He told me he had a film project that he wanted me to audition for. He told me I would be perfect for the role, and that he could get me an audition. The movie was supposed to be a biopic for the actress Lena Horne, and he thought it could be my big breakout role. My agent was in talks with getting me auditions and acting classes to make sure I would be taken seriously, and my first audition I killed it. I was told that some other big name actresses were going up for this role, but I was not intimidated. I knew I had the looks and the talent, and I knew the casting director had his eye on me. Brandon Morris was a black casting director who looked like a young Lawrence Fishburne from his 'What's Love Got To Do With It' days. He wasn't my type at all, but if I could flirt a little bit, maybe that could work in my favor. Throughout the rest of the casting process, I played into his eye for me. I was never expecting him to actually ask me out to dinner. The decision hadn't been made yet, so I could not say no. For me I had made up in my mind I was willing to do whatever it took to get this role. Luckily when I met up with Brandon that night for dinner his mind was on getting me an image and not fucking me. Brandon had told me I needed to start getting my name buzzing. He thought I was the best option, but they needed to build some publicity around my name. He gave me the number to a couple of gossip columnists and suggested I start selling some stories about myself and E. For me that was light work. I was ready to make calls the next morning. I know E was starting to wonder where these stories on us were coming from out of the blue. Of course I pretended to be clueless, but now I was on the cover of tabloids and gossip sites, and in a few weeks I would know if I had the role of my dreams. E and I had been having some amazing sex lately. The dick was so good, I wasn't even making sure he was wrapping it up every time. It didn't dawn on me until my period didn't come. I was too nervous to even take a pregnancy test. That would be the one thing that could ruin all my plans. I knew I would have to eventually find out the truth.

**TO BE CONTINUED...**

## *Twist Of Fate*

Author: Kiara Rashai

Alicia's heels picked up the pace as she walked briskly down the icy sidewalk. She had five inch heels on and desperately needed relief. She clutched her beige trench coat closely as she felt the wicked wind at her long, exposed legs. She giggled as she thought about her legs being exposed the night before.

Alicia's husband Edwin was in rare form. Alicia's legs were high in the air, spread as far as they could muster. Edwin was right in between them loving every drop that fell from her moist center. On top of their dining room table, Alicia was loving every minute of her bae pleasing her. Edwin had his right hand wrapped around Alicia's neck, slightly squeezing. The rush of being choked sent Alicia into overdrive.

"Yes! Right there" she yelled! Edwin lifted her right leg so that it was over his right shoulder. Never stopping the hold he had on his wife's neck, Edwin looked at his wife lovingly. Their stare was intense and Edwin panted almost in a pulse as he licked his lips and sucked his wife's foot.

"Oh, my goodness!" Alicia squealed in ecstasy. Edwin sucked and slobbered all over her big toe like it was a popsicle melting at rapid pace. Alicia couldn't contain herself.

"What the hell has gotten into you?!" She said clutching a fistful of her hair. The clamps on her nipples were making her torso tense.

"Please, E! Slow down!" She pleaded. Edwin never stopped his pace as he tightened his grip on Alicia's neck. Alicia's toes curled as she felt her body betray her. A warm sensation from her head down to her curled toes greeted her as she threw her head back that hung off the marble table.

"Yes! Yes! Yes!" Alicia coached. Edwin's chocolate six pack shined in the dim lit room as the sweat trickled down his abs. Alicia's high was at its peak as her muscles tightened and her hands were now tightly around Edwin's wrist that supported the hand that was helping Alicia reach her goal.

"Ugh, shit, I'm comin' too!" Edwin announced pounding as hard he could. Alicia's body lifted off the table. The legs of the table looked as if they were trying their hardest not to give up on the duo. Alicia screamed in ecstasy as her body began to come down from her high. Edwin collapsed on top of Alicia, his head nestled in between her thirty-six double D's. Planting kisses on his wife's chest and neck, he whispered his famous phrase, "I'm nothing without you. I love you." He said in between pants, trying to catch his breath. Alicia smiled as she ran a hand over his fresh fade haircut. "I love you to babe," she smiled. Even after fifteen years of marriage, the love still resonated with the couple. After the best love making they had ever made, they finally conceived their first child that they had wanted for over five years.

As the memory of the night before reminded her of all the good lovemaking, she totally forgot about the brisk winter wind that seemed to clutch her bones. Her Ralph Lauren mesh skirt was doing little to comfort her from the twenty-five-degree weather. It was eight o'clock at night exactly and Alicia was over the work day. As a paralegal, she was constantly on her feet, in and out of cars, trying to please her big-time lawyer boss. Peterson & Co., worked her endlessly, but he paid her handsomely. It was such a catch twenty-two. Desperate to unwind, she walked out of her usually twelve story building that she spent more than seventy hours a week at. As she started to walk down the usual lonely street, her trench coat flew up fighting the winter wind. Seeing her sapphire blue 2017 continental premiere car in her sights, she thanked the man above. The cold winter breeze tossed her burgundy hair behind her as she kept her impatient speed to get to her car. Suddenly, she heard footsteps behind her. Glancing behind her shortly, she saw no one. Never stopping the speed she accumulated, Alicia was within arm's length of her vehicle. Suddenly, Alicia felt a force pull her backward, and with a leather glove covered her mouth. Trying to scream, she fell on deaf ears as the assailant picked her up from the pavement.

"Shit! The gun!" She thought. Edwin had always instilled in Alicia the power of protecting herself. When they were in college, Edwin took Alicia to a gun range. Edwin wanted to make sure she knew how to shoot, when to shoot, and to feel comfortable protecting herself. The gold and black nine millimeter she ended up falling in love with, never left her side. However, at work, she wasn't allowed to bring it. She had no choice, but to keep it under the driver's seat of her car. She struggled to get free as she was carried to an abandoned building right across from her car.

"No! Please!" She cried, tears streaming down her face. The attacker threw her off his shoulder and onto the cold damp wood floor. Trying to kick her assailant between the legs with her five inch pumps angered her attacker. He immediately slapped Alicia as hard as he could. The masked attacker took zip ties and tied Alicia's arms and legs together. Alicia's eyes searched for anything she could pick up, but the house was so damaged that all she saw was faint fixtures and light snow covered most of the floor. Trying not to panic, she looked on as her attacker hovered over her almost unsure of what to do. Alicia tried to use this to her advantage, kicking her attacker as hard as she could where the person could feel in it in his soul, his testicles. Connecting, the kidnapper fell and Alicia rolled onto her stomach quickly, getting up from the damp floor. Quick on her feet, she kicked her shoes off and ran out of the house in the direction of her car. Hands zip tied, she knew it was a lost cause trying to flag down a taxi or unknown car. The street she was on was basically a ghost town. New York was expecting twelve to sixteen inches of snow that night and even higher in certain areas. The local mayor even suggested all traffic to cease after seven pm. Despite her best efforts to get into her car, she felt defeated with losing her car key and her wrists being tied. She began to run. Before she knew it, Alicia was pushed into a mountain of snow and a swift blow to the side of the head knocked her unconscious.

Unconscious for what felt like forever, Alicia finally came back to life. She was stripped of her clothes down to her matching corset bra and underwear. She was gagged and her arms and legs were tied to a bedpost by some sort of cloth. Alicia's hair was disheveled. She tugged at her bondage, but nothing happened. Her blurry vision began fixated on her surroundings. She was in a familiar room with black satin sheets and matching curtains. The room was decorated elegantly with tasteful art and sophisticated status. As she looked around more observantly, she noticed the room was dimly lit with tea cup candles. The floor around the bed was even surrounded by candles. The room smelled of vanilla and rose petals covered her intimate areas.

“Hello?” She asked to no one. The room was spacious and even seemed to swallow her voice up.

“Please! Please, just let me go!” Alicia pleaded, tugging at her bondages. The tugging did zilch to the stern cloth that seemed to fit like a glove around her wrists and ankles. Tears streamed down her face as she came to the realization that this moment was it. She would never get out of this room. She would never go back to her career, which she loved. Alicia began to think of her husband.

*“He must be worried sick.”*

He always waited for her to come home, rubbing her feet as soon as she came through the door. She cried harder thinking of all the times he’d come home early to give her flowers and run her a bath. She thought of all the times he cooked for her, even putting himself through culinary arts school just because he knew how much she loved food. She thought of all the times her husband made sure the kids were tucked in and read to while she could enjoy reading in her den or getting housework done. Moments of out of town trips flashed through her brain of the two. She shook her head and screamed as loud as she could. The room just echoed her screams. It felt like eternity when she finally heard the door squeak open. The dark figure appeared almost instantly and moved directly towards Alicia's helpless body. Alicia trembled as the tall figure took a blindfold out and covered her eyes.

"Please, don't hurt me," she cried out. The tall masked figure grabbed her neck slightly and began to squeeze a little at a time.

"No!" She screamed, struggling to break free of the hold. The figure squeezed harder cutting off Alicia's air supply. You could hear the echo of the struggle of gasps of air and screams. In almost perfect timing, the tall figure released its hold on Alicia's neck. Alicia coughed uncontrollably as she continued to break free of the hold that the figure had on her wrists and ankles.

"It's not going to work. Stop trying," the figure spoke carefully. Alicia's ears perked up at the sound of the figure's voice. '

*"What the hell is going on*?" She thought and once Alicia caught her breath, she tried to remain calm. It was one of the many things Edwin had taught her. Attackers feed off that fear. If you remain calm, they are more likely to figure out what your

thinking giving you more time," she could hear her husband say. Whoever was doing this, loved the reaction of her being helpless.

"Whatever you want, I can make sure you have it. There's a brand-new car outside. It's yours," Alicia said, but silence fell upon the room.

"I have money in my purse. Please. All of it is yours if you let me go," Alicia said pervasively and it was silence again. Alicia began to think she was only talking to herself. The figure turned around and walked out the room closing the door behind it. As soon as she saw the door close, she tried to bite at the bondages on her wrists. Loosening one side, she began to tug. Tired, she hung her head. Even though she was close to getting one side free, she was exhausted. Suddenly, she heard rapid footsteps. It was like someone was running. Her head perked up.

"HELP! PLEASE, HELP!!!" She screamed! Suddenly, the footsteps, ceased. Slowly, her breath became shallow. Just then, the bedroom door kicked open.

My chest felt like it was going to explode. "Edwin?! Edwin, baby, help me!!!" I screamed. Seeing his face allowed my body to relax a little. Edwin ran over to my barely covered body and planted kisses all over me.

“Oh my God sweetie! I am so sorry!” He pleaded releasing the gag. He took a pocket knife out of his pocket and cut my bondages. My wrists are swollen.

“What the hell is going on?! There’s this guy babe, he…”

"Shhhh. I got it,” Edwin said covering my body with a sheet. Tossing the sheet aside, I jumped in his arms and kissed him deeply. Kissing me back, Edwin palmed my behind picking me up. He gave me a half smile.

“What are you smiling at?” I asked. He placed me in a single chair that rested in the corner. Placing the sheet back on top of me, he turned around.

“Where are you going?” I asked.

“Edwin, this man just…”

"I got it, A….” Is all he said before leaving out the room.

“Edwin? Edwin?! E, don’t you dare fucking leave me!” I yelled. Ignoring my pleas, he left out of the room, locking it. I jumped out the chair and banged on the door.

"Edwin?! E?!" Jerking the doorknob there was a slight crack in the door, which meant there was something holding the door. Edwin had kicked the door open, so why was it locked? I looked in the crack. It was a clean look into the bare hallway.

"E?!" I yelled, but there was nothing except straight silence.

"Edwin?!" I yelled in frustration. After a moment of silence my instincts went into survival mode. I ran over to the curtains and pulled them back. The windows had steel bars attached to them. Looking around, I picked up the single sturdy chair and held it over my head. As I threw the chair, the bedroom door opened and glass shattered.

"Alicia!" The tall figured masked man yelled removing his mask. I dropped to my knees.

"What the fuck?! It was you?!" I said in disbelief. Edwin's best friend pulled out a forty caliber.

"Why?" I asked tearfully.

"Where's E?!"

"Right here," Edwin said behind his best friend. He had a silencer pointed directly at the back of his best friend's head.

"Don't make me do this, D!"

"Are you fucking kidding me?! You fuck my fiancé' and now I have to make sure YOU DON'T kill ME?!" Damon said with a slight chuckle.

"What?" I said tearfully. Barely unable to stand I used the wall as leverage.

"E, you..."

"Alicia, stay out of it!" Edwin yelled.

"Stay out of it?!" Damon laughed.

"You don't even know, do you?" Damon looked at me curiously. Swallowing hard, tears fell uncontrollably as I realized my world was crashing right before my eyes.

"Those kids you helped take care of, those are mine," Damon said nonchalantly.

Puzzled, I just ran my hands through my hair. "The fuck is he talking about Edwin?!" I said looking at my husband.

"SHUT THE FUCK UP, DAMON!"

"NO! She needs to know!"

"Know what?"

"Know that he fucked my wife for the last five years and she had his kids!" Was all I heard and then the silencer did its job. Damon had fallen right where he stood. Crying and shaking uncontrollably my legs gave out on me and I fell where I stood.

"W-W-Why? Why would you?"

"Three miscarriages, you and your attorney friend, it just was a lot and I didn't know…"

"You didn't know what?! Fuck you, Edwin?! All the sacrifices I've made for you?!"

"Sacrifices?! I put myself through school for you, I moved more than three thousand miles away from everyone I ever known. I fucked my best friend's wife so YOU could have the children you always wanted and I'm the bad guy?!"

"Edwin, don't put this on me!"

"It's all on you. You are about to take care of everything on your own, like you always wanted. I maxed out all our credit cards, the house is in foreclosure, and the car is in the river."

"W-What?"

"You wanted to take advantage of me. Make ME to look like the crazy one? Well, who's fucking crazy now, Alicia?!" Is all I heard before Edwin pointed the gun to his head.

"NOOOOOOOO!!!!" I screamed, but it was too late. In a matter of seconds, I had lost the only thing, I had ever known. Suddenly, black smoke had filled the room. As I looked at the lifeless bodies before me, it hit me that the life I created for myself was all smiles to public perception. To the outside, life was good. It was all happy pictures and countless beautiful memories. But, it really wasn't. My husband was having an affair. My kids weren't my step children and the man that I had known practically my whole life was someone else. So, what do you do? What do you do when you realized that your life is a lie? As the room covered with smoke and the flames reached the doorway, I laid completely flat. My stomach greeted the hard, cold, stained, wooden floor. A single tear fell down my cheek as I made my decision to live and die for the family I tried so very hard to create. When you are down on your luck, you must keep trying. My luck had ran out. The man that I loved and shared beds with, was now my companion down to the last moments of life. I was now with the house that me and Edwin had bought months earlier. I later found out this house was a cover-up for him to run narcotics out of. Nobody is who they appear and as the flames consumed the room and eventually me, I realized everyone has choices, but you need to be clear of what those are. Choices lead to lifelong consequences…

## ***Conversations On A Downtown Stroll***

Author: Cheraee C.

"I told this man Colton, I don't do criminals, felons, thugs, fugitives none of that hot boy ish."

Calice had a swifter clean record, she was blunt, and bougie, and it was nothing she wouldn't do for her husband Colton. Often Colton would take Calice out her element, and that was never a good thing, because she wasn't a people person.

"Now he got me downtown with all the courts, jails, non-driving assholes, creep squad affiliates, and five-o's looking like a little hypocrite."

Calice absolutely hated driving downtown just as much as she dreaded parking there. Parking was usually bumper to bumper and $50 in the AM and $5 in the PM. Downtown parking lots are the biggest hustle - scam ever. Calice found her some cheap $5 parking off the service drive, a few blocks away from the jail by Greektown Casino. This parking lot was the only parking lot she knew that wasn't guilty of price gouging.

As Calice was beginning her trail to the Frank Murphy Hall of Justice, a homeless man started yapping to her.

"Excuse me ma'am, do you got a slim jim?"

"Do I look like a gas station to you? You need to find you a Sunoco, a Citgo, a BP or something, and $.65. That's what you need to do. "

"I don't understand sarcasm so is that a yes or no?"

"It's a hell no and if you keep talking to me, I'm going to go to my car and pull that thang out on you."

"I just wanted a cigarette ma'am. Why you couldn't just be normal and say yes or no?"

"I'm not a polite person so go hound somebody else before my husband break out of jail and beat your ass."

"So you goin shoot me and get your locked up husband to beat my ass over a cigarette? Why would anybody want to marry you, your a mean lady?" Calice started speeding up and began walking faster. The homeless man was obviously looking for a cigarette and a friend.

Finally, Calice approached the courthouse. It was 7:52 AM. The doors were still locked shut and people were scattered around everywhere like we wasn't all about to have to get in one single file line. As Calice was standing there alone, a ghetto caramel skin lady came up to her touching her braids like she knew Calice from around the way or something.

"Your braids are flawless girl. Did the Africans do those?"

"Can you please stop touching my hair. I don't know you, and I don't know where your hands been."

"I swear west-side bitches don't know how to take complements these days."

"And I swear bitches should start treating other bitches like the strangers they are before they get they ass beat outside of Frank Murphy. It don't matter what side of town I'm from."

"I hope them braids pull out your hair and your edges."

"And I hope now that you see my hairstyle, you'll call your hair stylist right now and fire her. Get a new hair stylist, one that can actually slay hair then you won't have to go around harassing people's hair."

"You know what your braids are ugly as hell and your scalp is gasping for air! You have a nice day."

"I will have a nice day, matter fact I'm going to have a great day."

It was finally time to enter the building. These downtown folks were getting ridiculous and had no chill. Calice was really on the verge of snapping and going back home. She hoped nobody else felt like being sociable today.

After Calice made it past security and the security detectors, she went to the famous wall to find Colton's courtroom number. One of the security guards that were employed there decided to shoot his shot.

"What type of nigga got your fine ass down here? If you was my woman, I would never go to jail, I wouldn't even get a ticket."

"You should never say never. My husband is dealing with something old on his record because you downtown officials don't know how to process paperwork correctly."

"Well ain't nothing like these downtown restaurants. I would love to take you out to one."

"Your little security money can't do nothing for me baby that I can't do for myself. My husband gives me allowance $300 dollars a day. So I don't care what he does or doesn't do. He ain't never leaving me and I ain't never leaving him." Calice knew old boy would never be able to make a comeback after that.

"This ain't my only hustle baby girl. I got lots of hustles. When you get tired of being his wife come holler at me. I'm sure you'll be back down here. We'll cross paths again."

"Keep hope alive," Calice said headed for the elevators and pressing the button going up.

"I wonder is this how the inmates be in the county when they get a roommate. They just tell you they whole life story and never shut up."

Calice hopped on the elevator and went to the second floor. She found Colton's courtroom as soon as she got off the elevator and sat down at some seating right outside of it by a big picture window overlooking downtown. As she was sitting by the window a dark skinned girl started talking to her.

“You don’t look from around here,” the girl observed me.

"Neither do you, yet we both are sitting here for something."

"I told my man if he got arrested again, I was leaving him. He's been arrested like 100 times, and his record probably long as a 200 page book novel or longer."

"You know damn well your never going to leave him. I don't even know why your entertaining the thought."

"I told him this was the last time, and the last straw for me. I'm for real. He got to get his life together or get to stepping."

"You mine as well dump him now, because I bet you he goin have your ass right back down here within the next 30 days."

"What makes you so sure about that?"

"Men will always tell you what you want to hear and they will always tell you how they gonna change. I bet you he's been saying he was gonna change since you've known him."

"Girl, you is so right."

"I'm not your girl, I'm just putting you up on game."

"So what should I do?"

“Go home and don’t look back, let that little boy grow up. Real men don’t play games with your time or the justice system.”

“Your absolutely right, I’m about to go home. Thanks for the pep talk,” the girl got up and went to the elevators.

People were starting to enter the courtroom so Calice entered it to and found her a seat in the back. Armed robbery, assault with a deadly weapon, domestic violence, obstruction of justice, carjacking, DUI's, nothing but crimes, crimes, and more crimes. Calice felt like she was filming on an episode of Law and Order, sweating in the third row of Courtroom 234. She swore after today you couldn't pay her a million dollars to sit inside or outside another courtroom for anybody's case. Her virgin mind felt so heavy, violated, and disgusted at the lack of appreciation for dear life and justice. You couldn't tell her she wasn't in the presence of Michigan's Most Wanted that day.

Right or wrong it was a wives’ duty to be supportive. Once Colton’s case was up and the judge gave his ruling for his case, she was ghost. Out of nowhere, this chick sat next to Calice even though there were plenty of other seating where you could sit comfortably.

"Excuse me do you have some gum?" She asked trying to make conversation.

"No I don't like gum or candy."

"You been here for a long time?"

"I've been here since the courts opened. I like being punctual."

"Next rime girl you should come late or else you'll be waiting here forever. These judges take their precious time with these cases. They'll have you listening to everybody case in here like you the prosecutor."

"I see, are you here for somebody's case or do you work here?"

"I do need a job here as much as I be down here. So what your man do?"

"I don't have a man, I have a husband, and he didn't do anything. People downtown don't know how to process paperwork correctly."

"That's messed up, but you didn't have to shade us unmarried women like that."

"Well stop playing wifey and tell your man to put a ring on it. But you shouldn't have to tell your man to do nothing. If you've been rocking with him like you said you have, I would've been put a ring on it and a last name on it."

"I had an engagement ring before, but we pawned that bad boy at American Jewelry & Loan for a bail bondsman at A-1 Bails Bond in case you ever need a referral for a bail bondsman. I know it's a bunch of them in the yellow pages, but trust me, you'll be a year trying to find a good one. But, we stay in debt, and he stay in trouble so we just let it go to the pawn shop."

"So you never got another ring and he never married you after you have shown him such undying loyalty?"

"Nope."

"Excuse me, I got to go use the restroom." That was it. Calice tried her hardest to mind her own business on so many occasions, but people just wouldn't stop conversating with her. Nothing about Calice's face said "friendly" or "talk to me." Calice headed for the stairs, forget the elevator. She wished she had a big hat and some dark sunglasses so she could exit the building in peace. Checking the perimeter, Calice didn't see nobody in sight that she talked too that day so she practically ran to the exit door. When she hit the street, she practically darted to her car. Once she was safe in her car and had locked all her doors she took a deep sigh of relief. She knew she was going to hear Colton's mouth later for not being at his court hearing.

*"Oh well, peace out downtown, I'm going home where I belong. Colton shouldn't have got in this mess and he would be at home too."*

## *The Voice of Addiction*

Author: Black Goddess Sable

I go by many products. The world thinks they have me all figured out, but in the end they get more confused. See they think a therapist and treatment will make me go away, but i got these fools wrapped around my finger. You poor simple fools, do you really think you can get rid of me that easy? Don't you know i am a parasite, I need my host to survive. Anything that happens to me affects the host. So go ahead ,try to get rid of me, keep me from him/her, but I promise you it won't do you any good. I am abused on the streets, in prescriptions, and in the hospitals. So don't kid yourself, if you think you can get rid of me with a snap of your fingers. Doctors use me for money and to escape their lives, not realizing they are in my web, until they're about to lose their licenses. The power I have over people is phenomenal. I love high-jacking the host, making them do things they`ve never done before. I can make them beg on the streets, be homeless, a stripper, a cheater, a deadbeat parent, drop out of school, lose their job, and abandon the ones they love. I am so powerful that even if you try to get rid of me, the host suffers withdraws and wishes they were dead. I am so powerful that I can make my host vomit, constipated, lose weight, break into a cold sweat, give them a heart attack, and cause blackouts. I am so powerful I can keep a host from breathing. I control every aspect of the host's life. The only way to get rid of me is for the host to die. Since we both don't want that, I will just stick around. You see I run the mind, you can't get rid of me, I am in your head. I provide the best high and escape from reality compared to a man or a woman. I am better than sex, family, and friends. Once you try me, your friends will disown you, your family will cast you out, your lover won't understand you, you will be spit upon, hated, feared, but most of all you will be alone. That's where I come in and soothe your pain. Just one taste and you will never want to come back. I will accept you, never judge you, never hate or remind you of your past. I can give you wealth beyond your wildest dreams, I can give you men/women that will do anything for you, I will never hurt you, and most of all I will never leave you.

## *Surviving the Devil*

Author: Ice

As I sit and look into this dirty mirror in this dirty ass motel room, I don't recognize the person staring back at me. How did I allow myself to get into this predicament? All the books in the world couldn't and didn't prepare me for what I've endured the past 17 years. Look at me, all bruised and battered. My hair looks a mess and my clothes are ripped and bloody. The signs were there, red flags everywhere!!! I should've ran for the border but no, I decided to have a family and stay. Silly me. Now all I have to do is figure out how the hell am I going to get rid of this body laying on the floor. My name is Sky and this is how it all began.

### *Summer 2001-August*

Riding down Chicago Avenue, me and my girl Marlena was kicking it, sipping Henny, and bumping Pac "All Eyes On Me" album. We got caught by a red light when she turned down the music in my ride.

"Girl wait a minute! Did you see how he was eyeballing me and undressing me with his eyes?" Marlena said.

"Yes! I was creeped out for you!" I said.

"The whole time I was braiding his hair and turning his head, he kept turning to look back over at you." We bust out laughing.

A brown and gold old school Delta 88 pulled up on the side of us at that moment and we both peeked over to see who was in there. He was watching us with piercing eyes. Kind of like the guy whose hair I was just braiding was looking at Marlena. So I looked him dead in his eyes and rolled mines, and turned my head. He honked his horn and reached over to roll his window all the way down.

"How y'all doing?" He asked. I looked at her because he couldn't have been talking to me because I just gave him the nastiest eye roll in the world. We laughed and the light turned green as he yelled, "aye pull over real quick!"

Against my better judgment I pulled over to the gas station right in front of us. He got out of the car and came over to my car on my side. I tried not to laugh because Marlena crazy ass was whispering, "oh he on you girl." We kicked it for a brief second, I gave him my house number, and I pulled off never to think about it again. Hell I gave him that number because I was never really home anyway. We rode around for about another hour before I took her to her boo house and headed home. I lived with my mother Annette. Everybody called her Peaches and my little sister Candy which was short for Candice.

"Hey baby," my mama said as soon as I opened the side door. I didn't want her to smell the weed or the liquor on me so I stayed by the side door. Although I was 18 and legal and she knew what I did, I still didn't want to hear her damn mouth about not being grown.

"Hey mama, what you doing still up?" I asked her while fidgeting with the locks and taking my shoes off.

"Getting something to drink and I just looked out the window and seen your car. So I waited for you to make it in the house safely," she said as she turned to go in her room. I tried to hurry up and beeline to my room fast as I could when I heard her yell, "and don't bring your ass in here like that no more!" It scared the hell out of me when she yelled and I tripped up the stairs. When I finally made it in my room and took off my clothes I laid down on the bed and laughed.

"How the hell was she always on point?" I said to myself about my mama. Man she be on it. I was planning on watching Jerry Springer's late night show until Calgon took me away when my house phone rang. I was going to let it ring because who in the hell was calling me this late. It was past midnight, but whoever it was let the damn phone keep ringing.

"Hello!" I said obviously irritated.

"Hi, can I speak to Sky? The man on the other end of the phone asked.

"Who is this?" I asked looking at the phone, laying back down on my bed.

"It's Rocko."

"Rocko who?"

"The guy you just met at the gas station tonight." I turned my nose all the way up. First of all you calling me late and secondly damn I just gave you my number and your calling already. I thought to myself.

"Oh ok, what up doe?" I replied kinda not interested.

"Nothing much, did I catch you busy?" He asked and I thought does it really matter?

"Actually I was about to go to bed, but what's up?" We talked for about an hour and he said he would call me when he got to work in the morning. I agreed and went straight to sleep. The next morning like clockwork he was right on time and called while he was at work. We agreed to hang out later that day and go to the movies. I told him I was going to bring my girl Marlena since I didn't know him like that. He said he was going to bring his boy and they would be at my house around 7:00 pm. I scooped Marlena up around 5:00 pm just so we could get a game plan together in case these niggas started acting crazy on us. We got dressed at my house since that's where they were coming to.

"Ok so do you have your pocket knife?" I asked her while putting on my lip gloss and liner.

"You know I do," she said pulling her knife out of her back pocket flicking the blade out.

"Ok, cool! I got my shit too!" I pulled my knife out of the side of my half bra.

My mama was due to come home from work around 7:30 pm and the boys were supposed to be there soon so we had to hurry up. I didn't want my mama to give them the third degree like she did all of my guy friends. Hell even the ones she knew I grew up with she grilled the hell out of them too. Mama must have gotten off early because when I heard those keys, giggling, I looked at the clock and it was 6:50 pm. When she walked in the door she started ranting about a car full of niggas sitting out in front of her house. *Oh shit, I knew it was on then.*

"Sky!! Who is those muthafuckas sitting in front of my house?" She asked putting her purse down on the couch and standing in the door looking at them still sitting in the car.

"Um, oh that's our friends' mama. We're about to go to the movies," I said coming to the door. She looked at me and Marlena up and down and rolled her eyes.

"Y'all wearing that to the movies huh?" She pointed and scanned our outfits some more. I was wearing a red halter top and some short black shorts and Marlena had on a halter top with some tight fitted jeans. She kept going with her flow.

"And these little niggas have no manners and no damn respect. They couldn't even come greet y'all at the door!"

Knocking at the door was a big thing with my family. It showed signs of respect and you sure as hell bet not pull up and blow the horn. Mama always said, "you blow for hoes and wasn't no hoes in her house."

"The fact that they see me looking at them and still have yet to get out of the car and make a move towards the house is a big strike," she said and slammed the door shut.

As soon as she headed to the bathroom to run her bath water, I opened the door and flicked the porch lights to get their attention. Once Rocko looked up, I waved for him to come up to the house. Rocko got out the car, but his boy stayed behind. I let him in and my mama bent that corner and let his ass have it. Straight ice grilled him. She checked his identification and even went outside to get his boy license plate number. He looked shook, but he held his composure.

"I don't expect this to be an all night long thing Sky," mama said as we started to head out.

Her thing had always been she didn't care how old you were, as long as you stayed in her house you played by her rules. If you weren't in her house by 2:00 am, stay wherever the hell you were at. She didn't play that coming in all types of night.

"Ok mama, it won't be." We dipped out quick as hell before she could start interrogating the nigga about his parents and all type of other shit. We hit the liquor store up the street from my house on Plymouth and Pierson. Although me and Lena was only 18, we drunk and smoked just like the old folks and could hang with the best of them. Rocko was 21 and his boy Doe was 22 so they were able to cop the drink with no problem. They grabbed a fifth of Remy 1738 and we rode. I could tell that Doe was really feeling Lena, but I already knew she was all in with her nigga so shit wasn't going nowhere far, but this car. She had been with him since middle school so no matter who they fucked with on the side, they were down for each other and stayed together. Instead of hitting the movies we opted to ride around, drink, smoke, and listen to music. Kind of get to know each other a little better. Everything went smooth and we ended the night playing like we had something important to do in the morning. They dropped us back off and the rest was history.

Me and Rocko spent damn near every day after that together. He wasn't my type at first, but it was something about him that I wanted to get to know more about and he had my attention for the moment. I would spend the night at his sister's apartment with him on the weekends and go home on Sunday morning. We weren't fucking yet, but he was sure trying to apply pressure every time I was over there.

One day he asked me to come over his mama house where he actually stayed. I only had one class left to go to that day so I said fuck it and went over there. Everything was everything, we hit it off and got it in that day. He even asked me to be his girl and I said. "yes." Right after we finished we heard some keys in the door. Luckily we were just sitting on the floor watching TV at that moment.

"Who the hell is this?" This short bald headed guy asked while pointing at me.

"This is my friend," Rocko said.

I could tell by the look on dude face he was not feeling me being there. He stared at us for a few more seconds then walked off and headed upstairs. Minutes later you could hear him on the phone with somebody talking about how he don't want nobody in his house. I started grabbing my shit to go and Rocko grabbed my arm.

"Go wait in the living room," he said and went upstairs.

I stood in the living room feeling uncomfortable hearing them argue. I just stood there looking around. It was pictures of this cute little girl hanging on the walls all dressed up. So I started examining them and the other I to try to take my mind off of them upstairs. Just then he came rushing down the stairs.

"Let's go!" He yelled grabbing my arm leading me outside. When I got in my car he told me to meet him at his sister house, got in his ride, and peeled out. That was the day he got put out and moved in with his sister in her one bedroom apartment. Hell he was over there most of the time anyway so he might as well have lived there.

"Who's baby was that in the pictures on the wall?" I asked trying to break the awkward silence that was between us while we sat on the couch at the apartment.

"Oh that's my niece." He said it so quick and nonchalantly I believed it. I knew he had a brother that was locked up so I figured it was his daughter because his sister didn't have any kids.

"She's pretty," I said.

"Thank you."

We smoked a blunt and kicked it for a minute about us and what happened at the house earlier.

“Man that nigga always be tripping!” Rocko said.

“I see. Dude was on tip.”

“He don’t be wanting nobody over at his house thinking somebody is going to steal from his ass. My mama bought 90% of all the shit in that house any damn way,” he said smacking his teeth. We both laughed.

Months had passed and we were at the apartment chilling and cooking. His sister was rarely home. She was always working or at her nigga house. My pager went off so I checked it. Normally I would have a burn out phone, but the one I had just got hit so I had to wait for the next shipment to come in. I grabbed some change from my purse to use the Pay phone right outside the building.

“Where you about to go?” He asked.

“Lena just paged me 911. I’ll be right back I’m about to see what’s up with her.”

In the hallway his boy Pig was coming up the stairs as I was going down.

“What’s good shorty?” Pig said hitting his blunt.

“Shit, you about to go to the apartment or you going home?”

“Naw, I’m about to go to my house and then probably stop by there on my way back out.”

"What's up?" He asked.

"Leave me a bag with him please." I reached in my pocket, gave him a ten, and kept it pushing. One and a half rings and Lena answered the phone.

"What's up girl?" I asked leaning up against the pay phone.

"Girl! Me and B just got into it harder than a muthafucka!" She started yelling through the phone. I could tell she had been crying and yelling by the way. Her voice was hoarse.

"Oh hell naw. For what!?"

"Bitch, I went over there and this nigga was having a party. The house was full of people, niggas and bitches. I had been knocking on the door for a minute and didn't get an answer because the music was blasting." I could hear her sparking up something as she paused. I started thinking like damn I should've grabbed my cigarettes because I could tell shit was
about to get deep.

"Ok and so what happened?" I was anxious to know at this point.

"So I go to turn the knob and it's unlocked so I go in. I hear these nitches laughing and shit. Walk all the way in and they having their own little strip party. So I look around for him and don't see his ass nowhere."

"Oh shit!" I yelled scaring this lady walking past. I turned and put another quarter in the phone.

"Yeah exactly. I headed to his room and he got some broad in there sucking his dick!"

At that moment my whole mouth dropped. He done lost his mind. This was all bad. She continued telling me how he tried to play it like it wasn't what she thought she saw. How the girl was on her knees because she was looking for her earring that she'd lost when she put on a private show for one of the fellas, so he took her up there to look for it. Lena was far from stupid and was not buying that shit at all and I didn't blame her. We talked for 10 more minutes and I told her I would be through there later when I left him. As I was walking back to the apartment entry door, a car full of niggas in an old school Monte Carlo pulled over trying to holler. I paid their asses no mind and went inside. When I got to the apartment all hell broke loose.

"Who the fuck were you outside talking to all this time?!" He asked yelling in my face. He grabbed me and threw my back against the door.

"What the fucck is wrong with you nigga?! You better get your fucking hands off of me!" I screamed at him while giving his ass the stare down of death. This nigga marbles must have been scrambled because when I pushed him back off of me, he grabbed my damn neck.

"Dawg I'm not fucking playing with you! You out there talking to one of your niggas being disrespectful!"

I instantly started swinging, Not giving a fuck what I hit. He had me completely fucked up if he thought I was about to play those type of games. We fought for what seemed like forever and he pinned me down so I could stop swinging, like I was the problem. When he let me up I started getting my stuff. Rocko grabbed my pager that had fell on the floor while we were fighting and threw it so hard against the wall it shattered into pieces.

Pause...Now the story behind my pager is that it used to belong to my cousin Toto. Although me, my sister, and my cousins were raised like brothers and sisters, Toto was more like a father figure to me. I looked up to him so when he died a major piece of my whole family died with him. So to say the least fucking up that pager was like doing harm to my cousin. Okay I'm back...

"Bitch have you lost your mind!?" I screamed and charged at him blacking out. We started fighting again, this time I was crying and swinging, crying and swinging. I left and drove off.

"I swear to God I'm going to have them come fuck this bitch up!" I said to myself while driving down Joy Road about to go to the hood.

The Craft is where me and my family resided. I was born and raised on the Craft. I pulled up to my granny's house where my cousin Wood and friends were outside on the side of the house smoking and drinking per usual. When I hopped out the car he could see that I was heated and had been crying.

"Fuck wrong with you cuz?" He asked walking towards me.

I told him what had just happened and he said he would handle it. He gave me some cash to go replace my pager, but not before giving me a lecture about holding onto things that would eventually break or get old anyway and it wouldn't bring that person back. I wasn't trying to hear all of that. Although I seen his point, I was still livid. I was happy I could go get another pager, but I wanted him to feel my pain. Needless to say I went straight to the Page-tel and got another one. Low and behold as soon as they activated it this punk ass nigga was blowing my shit up. All I could think was why in the hell was he paging me after the bitch ass move he just pulled? *Naw fuck boy, you ain't getting no love this way*. I put my pager on my hip and went to bend a few corners. I went by my auntie's house to see if my phones had come yet.

"Hey boo," my Auntie Angie yelled from the porch as I killed the engine and got out.

"Hey auntie." I looked around at my cousins running up and down the block with their friends. My sister came out of the house with my auntie's dog Pepper on his leash.

"Hey Pepperoni!" I yelled and he ran over to me as I called him by his nickname I gave him. All of the kids couldn't stand Pepper ass, but they loved him though. He was a true spoiled brat to say the least and was a menace to the household whenever my auntie turned her back. She thought her little baby could do no wrong. He would piss up against the side of the stove so the kids would have to clean it up and get cussed out because she thought they didn't take him outside. He would bite them whenever he would get mad and piss on their personal stuff.

I remember this one time when we all went to ABC Warehouse, Pepper included, along with all of the kids. The Caravan was packed and of course Pepper wanted to stretch out like a king. My sister must've made a mistake and stepped on his tail because he tried to bite her. It was on like popcorn. Candi jumped out the van so quick and called his ass out like he was a fucking human and a nigga off the street. To make matters even worse my little cousin Gino starting egging her on screaming, "get him Candi, get him!" Like she was really about to throw hands with this damn dog.

My auntie kept yelling, "you better not hit my dog!" Candi wasn't trying to hear none of that. It was at that point I believed that my Auntie Angie could have got the hands to if she tried to stop Candi.

"Where are y'all about to go?" I asked Candi while the other kids started coming back to the house.

"We about to go for a walk," my cousin Nae answered. They dipped off down the street with Pepper bad ass in toe. All of them together, they were menaces to society. They were bad as hell, but knew how to act when it mattered.

"Did a package come for me auntie?"

"Yeah and your ass better stop sending that shit here too. Fuck around and get caught messing with them burnouts," she said and hit her cigarette.

"Let me get one of them," I said with my hand out she gave me one and I started telling her about the Rocko bullshit.

"What the fuck!" I turned around to see my other Auntie Lisa standing in the door.

"Hey auntie."

"Don't hey auntie me! Where that little bitch ass nigga at?" She asked coming out of the door.

"Shit I don't know and don't care, but he keep blowing my pager up."

"Call his ass and have him come over here. I got something for his ass!" She said in a matter of fact type of way, so I knew she wasn't playing. See my Auntie Lisa, out of all of my mama siblings ran with a gang of hardcore muthafuckas. Don't get me wrong every last one of them had that street mentality and will fuck somebody up quick. But with Lisa, one call and it was all over for whoever.

My granny had five kids, Dreana, Lisa, Annette, John, and Angie, in that order. Dreana was the most leveled headed one I believe out of the bunch. I always found myself talking to her about any and everything when I couldn't talk to my mama about it. She'd give me the real every time, straight no chaser. Don't get it twisted though she would pop off at any given moment if she needed to and she was just as lethal as the rest of them.

"Naw auntie, I'm going to just leave his ass alone. I don't have time for none of that."

"Yeah ok! One call and his ass is grass," she said thumping her cigarette into the yard. I knew she wasn't bullshitting either.

Out of all my relationships I've never had to get physical with any of them. Hell most of them didn't even get past first base with hitting this let alone hitting me. Even when they made me mad over little shit I just dipped and did not return. This nigga truly had me fucked up. I was done and over him or so I thought. After a few weeks went past with him stalking me at my people house, leaving his stuff in my car at my cousin house to let me know he was there, and continuously trying to reach out with his apologies, I fell for it and took him back. Biggest fucking mistake!

### *2003-February*

Me and Rocko had been doing good. I mean just like any other relationship, we had our disagreements and falling outs, but nothing major and nothing physical. He stayed in some type of bullshit in the streets though and I wasn't too fond of that. From popping pills on the regular, smoking weed and drinking, to selling dime bags of weed, and hanging with niggas who was always robbing niggas, you name it he was in it. I just didn't want shit to come back to him while I was with him, so I started to put a little distance in between us. We only really seen each other when I went over to the apartment. We never hung out anywhere because he hated the fact that everywhere we went I knew somebody from school or the hood. He was very insecure. He would immediately think that if it was a guy, I was fucking him or had fucked him. If it was a female I probably fucked her people or we were on some hoe shit together like I was just a hoe out here in these streets for real.

One day while I was over my auntie's house talking to my Uncle John, he called over there to see what I was doing.

"Hello," I said into the phone knowing it was him from the caller id.

"What you doing bay?"

"Over my auntie house, what's up?" I was dry as hell.

"Oh ok. Yeah I just rode past there and seen your car in the driveway." *He's a damn stalker I said to myself.*

"So if you rode by then you know what I'm doing and where I'm at." Now I was visibly irritated.

"I was just seeing what you had up and if you wanted to go rent some movies later and kick it."

"That's cool. We can do that. I'll call you later." I hung up the phone not giving him a chance to reply. I looked over at my uncle who was laughing.

"What's funny?"

“Honey, you are! You are something else. You remind me so much of my damn sisters. Them heffas don’t know how to act when they all in with a man or in love.”

I laughed, “I love him, but it’s not that deep.”

“Yeah, yeah I have heard all of that before,” he said and kept laughing.

“What you think he’s going to say and how he’s going to act when you tell him that you are pregnant?” My head turned so quick.

“Pregnant!? Who pregnant!? Ok now your tripping.” Now I was laughing even harder at him.

“Ok you think it’s funny now, but we will see.” I brushed what he said off and headed out to go get Lena for a minute before I hooked up with him. *Pregnant, shid not me.*

Now let me take you back to last year real quick. You remember the little girl who was in the pictures at his mama house right? Well yeah it turns out that it wasn’t his brother’s little girl and like I said his sister didn’t have any kids, it was his daughter!! Yeah that dirty muthafucka lied and denied his child. I never even thought more into the situation after that day until the day I was at the apartment doing his sister hair and chilling. She was going down memory lane showing me pictures of her when she was in high school and her family.

"This was me when I was in high school when my mama sent me down south to stay with my grandma," Cassie said showing me the picture.

"Oh ok, I see you with the asymmetrical cut," I said hyping her up.

"Girl yes, I was hot shit back then. I had the niggas all on me. My grandma tried to keep me tamed, but it didn't work." She flipped through a few more pages and there she was, that same little girl. She stopped and stared at the picture for a minute.

"She is so cute," I said.

"That's my baby. I gotta make a trip down there soon to see her."

"Oh ok where is she at?" I never had gotten any information on her whereabouts from Rocko.

"She's in Mississippi with my grandma. Grandma is getting to old to take care of her so eventually we are going to have to go get her." She said that like I already knew what was up. I kept probing because I figured something had to be up. Why would his brother whom they didn't share the same mother, have his baby down there with their grandma?

"Why is she down there with y'all grandma? His brother's family couldn't take her in while he did the bid. Damn that's messed up."

"Why would his brother's people take her in? She asked me confused.

"Nigga because that's his daughter!" I said.

"Girl that's not Zoo's daughter!" She said laughing while sparking up the blunt that had took her thirty minutes to surgically gut and roll. At this point I had to grab my drink and take a seat. Now this shit wasn't rocket science and I knew she had other siblings in Mississippi, but I wasn't sure of the connection that her daddy's family had with her mother's.

"So your brother on your daddy side let your grandma on your mother side take his baby in and raise her?" Now I was really confused and this was some freaky shit.

"Girl no! My brother don't have no kids and neither do my little sister. That's Rocko's daughter Sky."

I sat there for a minute to let that shit marinate. This scumbag ass muthafucka had lied to me about having kids. Not that it would've mattered, shit I love kids, but he said it was his niece. What type of piece of shit would lie about his seed?

"Oh ok," was all I could muster to get out as I sat there still shocked.

"Wait, you didn't know?" She asked me.

I didn't want to look any more foolish than I already did so I replied, "yeah girl I forgot he mentioned something like that when we first met." She went on to telling me about how him and the child's mother were young and stupid and how she had to take care of both of them and their baby. She told me about how they got into it big time and the girl took the baby and went down south. She dropped the baby off to his grandma, and went to Memphis so she could finish school and get herself together. The shit I had just heard had instantly gave me a headache. I finished her hair and took my ass home.

On the way home I couldn't do anything, but think about how he lied and how could anybody live with themselves after abandoning their child. I was on Chicago just passing the French Quarter Apartments when my car started acting up and cut off after a few tries, and it would not start back up. I called a cab to get home. I could've called Rocko, but I was not trying to see that lying sack of shit face.

The next day Rocko was blowing my phone up, I still hadn't answered or talked to him so he didn't know I was pissed and his little secret was out. I had to go to work so I had my mama drop me off. I was going to worry about my car later when I got off and I wasn't about to let this mess with Rocko mess up my day. After work I started walking to my auntie's house on Outer Drive which was right up the street from my job. He called me several times before I decided to pick up. I just didn't want his ass to pop up on me and especially not at my auntie's crib.

"What the fuck do you want Rocko?" I yelled into the phone.

"What's wrong with you?"

"Nigga, you're what's wrong with me! You are a real low life ass nigga. How could you deny your seed?!" I screamed through the phone.

"What are you talking about?" He asked playing dumb.

"Really! I asked you from the gate did you have any kids and you said no, right? Only to find out the little girl in the pictures is your child! Your deadbeat ass has the nerve to abandon her, deny her, and don't take care of her!" I hung up, it wasn't nothing his trifling ass could say to me. I found it then and still find it now to be disgusting – a person who doesn't properly take care of something they created. Kids don't ask to be here or go through none of the foul shit that they endure in a dysfunctional household.

Back to the current situation at hand. I started telling Lena the jokes my uncle had that day and we laughed about it.

"Maybe you should take a test just to be on the safe side," Lena suggested while passing me the blunt.

"Bitch! I'm not pregnant," I shook my head and turned the music up.

A few days later my uncle died. I was crushed, we were close. He had taught me everything I knew about hair. He was a bomb ass stylist and could sew his ass off. My uncle didn't have any kids of his own, he was gay. Although he always said he was gonna find the baddest bitch and have a baby with her, he never got a chance to. So he passed all of his skills surrounding hair to me, his oldest niece since I was always watching him anyway. The day after he died, me and Lena was riding while I laughed and cried reminiscing on the good times with my uncle and family.

"Aye you know what? They say when you lose a life you gain a life," she said.

"Don't start that shit! Not today Lena."

"I'm just saying Sky, you should really consider taking a test. John might've known something we don't."

"He was just talking shit like usual," I sighed. What if it was true? What if he knew something that I didn't and he knew he was about to leave us? Needless to say I reconsidered and we got a test from the dollar store. We went to my house to take the test.

Moments later, "what the fuck?" I screamed when I read the results.

"What?" Lena came rushing into the bathroom to see what was up.

"Bitch, this has got to be broken or something. Or maybe because it's cheap it's not accurate." She looked down at the test on the sink.

"Oh my God Sky!"

"Naw dawg that can't be right," I said shaking my head.

"Ok, so let's go get another one then," she said.

"Your tripping! I'm not pregnant and that cheap ass test don't mean shit."

"Look I took the same test and it said I was pregnant and I was, but we can go get another test from CVS and see what it says, and then go from there."

"I just want to chill man, this can't be true."

We went to the CVS around the corner from my house and got another test. This test had two of them in there and best believe I planned on taking both of them. How in the hell did this happen I thought to myself? I called myself taking a break from the depo shot and end up pregnant. Marlena just stared at me looking for a reaction as I stared at the test results.

"It's not all bad Sky. I mean consider this a blessing from John."

"Yeah I know. Man I'm not even really tripping off of being pregnant, I'm tripping off the fact of being pregnant by the cornball. He don't even have nothing to do with his daughter."

The possibilities of Rocko being an active parent in this kid's life was slim to none. I mean he left his daughter for somebody else to take care of her. I hadn't spoken to him since the other day and didn't plan on it, but she convinced me to call him to tell him what was up. I told him I would meet him at his night job where him and his mama Bertha cleaned the buildings out in Bingham. When I made it there him and Bertha was getting their carts to start cleaning heading towards the elevator.

"Hey Sky," his mama said.

"Hey, how are you?"

"Tired and ready to go already. I'll be glad when I can stop working both jobs. My body is getting tired."

"Let's make this quick because I have shit to do later tonight ma," Rocko said putting his cart on the elevator. We all got on and off on the same floor.

"So what's up?" He asked as soon as we were by ourselves.

"I'm pregnant," I said getting straight to the point.

"What? How?"

"Nigga how else?"

"I mean I know that, but I thought the shot was still in your system." He just stared at me.

"Me too, but apparently not. So what are we going to do?" I asked him with all seriousness.

"Shit I don't even have my daughter and right now I'm not in a position to get or have another baby."

"So what are you trying to say?" Hand on my hip, I meant business.

"Your going to have to get rid of it."

"You knew the consequences when we were doing what we were doing and you know how I feel about abortions because we talked about it."

Although having a baby wasn't part of my plan right now, I damn sure wasn't playing with the option of killing my baby.

"Yeah I know, but you aren't ready either." *The nerve of this nigga to tell me what I was ready for.*

"I'll pay for it just let me know how much it is," he said.

His mama came over to where we were in the middle of our conversation. She could sense the intensity by the look on my face.

"What's wrong?" She asked.

"Nothing," he quickly replied.

"Oh it's something alright," I said looking at him upside his head.

"Sky, what's wrong?" She turned and asked me.

"I'm pregnant."

"What?!" She looked as if she was mad, but for what I didn't know, but at the end of the day it was me and him that laid down together not her. She went on to talking about how he didn't need to be having a baby right now, the current situation with his daughter, and how she wasn't about to be taking care of another kid because he was irresponsible.

"You don't have to take care of nothing this way Bertha. You didn't lay down with me, he did."

"Yeah, but you need to realize neither one of y'all can take care of a baby." I mean really who was she to tell me what the fuck I could take care of? *Naw girlfriend you just need to worry about that little girl down south that all of y'all deadbeat muthafuckas left behind and not mine, I thought.*

"I'll figure it out and don't worry neither of y'all have to deal with me or this baby." I got on the elevator and left. The fact that they thought they could debo me into what they wanted me to do because of his previous fuckups had my mind gone. I couldn't wait to get home and tell my mama about the baby and this.

Mama wasn't too happy about me being pregnant and all with me still in school, but she was a hell of a lot more supportive than I thought she would be.

"Fuck them. We don't need them and neither do this baby," she said.

This nigga had come over to the hose to talk to me and my mama wouldn't let him because she didn't want me to get upset.

"I'm telling you if she don't get an abortion I'm going to kill myself in her trunk," he told my mama.

"Well do what you have to do muthafucka! It's her body, her decision."

"Ok which one you think is going to hurt her more? Her having the vision of me dead in her trunk or her getting an abortion?"

"You have got to be the stupidest nigga alive. You don't know what type of trauma she will go through killing her baby for you! She will be taking all types of risks. I tell you what, you can get the fuck off of my porch and don't look back. She'll call you when she's ready to talk." I heard the door slam.

Mama came upstairs and told me the conversation they had just had as if I wasn't on the stairs listening. The next day I went to the little center on 7mile for women to take another test and to see how far along I was. Eleven weeks and four days! Damn and I didn't have a clue. I had a real life baby growing inside of me. Rocko's no good ass brother finally got out of jail. I called him no good because of all the stories Cassie had told me. She low key seemed like she was feeling the nigga the way she kept talking about all of his hoes he had and spitting venom on him. When he caught wind of me being pregnant he had the audacity to offer Rocko the money for me to get the damn abortion.

"I tell you what, give me the money. I'll get it and you don't ever have to call me or see me again and I mean that shit from the bottom of my heart," I told Rocko.

Somewhere in my words to him he must've knew I wasn't playing because he didn't speak another word of abortion to me. Now what he was telling his people didn't have shit to do with me. I went to pick his brother up one day to take him to get some clothes to wear to see his PO and he got in the car talking.

"What's good sis?"

"Shit I can't call it. So where am I taking you?" I asked him trying to cut all the small talk out.

"Um can you take me to Marshalls on Middlebelt and 96?"

"Yea," I answered dryly. I just wanted to go eat and get in my bed.

"This stanking ass bitch didn't want to take me. She mad at me because my other bitch called her phone."

"Oh wow," I said not really interested in his issues.

When we pulled up to Marshalls I was going to stay in the car until he kept asking me to get out because he wanted a woman's opinion on what to get. So I finally slid out the car almost six months pregnant and pulled my shirt down.

"What the fuck?! You still pregnant?" He asked.

"Well it appears that way doesn't it?" I said and started walking past him.

"Man I gave that nigga the money to handle that!"

"Excuse me?!"

"I said I gave bro the money so you could get the abortion. I guess you spent that money on other shit huh?" *Ok so this nigga got me fucked up too. He don't know me from a can of paint and he flapping his gums.*

"I don't know what your brother told you, but I told him to give me the money, and I'll get it, and I was done with his ass."

He started talking all of the same shit that his mama and sister was talking. The same shit I didn't give two fucks to hear. I politely flipped him the bird and walked back to my car and left that bitch standing there in the parking lot. He called his brother and he called me, but I refused to be disrespected! *Bitch you need me, not the other way around.*

I guess me leaving his brother didn't sit right with Rocko because I had went from almost going back from shit to sugar to diarrhea. His car had broke down so he was using my car to get around which I didn't mind as long as I got to my appointments and handled my business. I had an appointment this morning at 8:30am and here it is 7:45am and he wasn't answering his phone. By the time he got to me I was pissed and super late for my appointment.

"My bad bay I had to take my brother to see his PO." Here he goes with the lame ass excuses.

"So your telling me you are late because of some shit you had to do for another nigga in my damn car?!"

"You acting like you still can't go to the appointment."

"Nigga I can't, I'm going to have to reschedule, give me my keys."

"Ok well since you rescheduling I can keep the car for a minute," he said going back towards the car.

"No I can drop you off and you can figure it out from there. I have things to do."

I got in the driver seat and reached for the keys, when he got in.

"You not about to drop me off. If anything you can take me to the places I have to go."

"No you should have been done all what you had to do while you had my car." I tried to take the keys out his hand. We started arguing and before I knew it he was snatching at the wheel and I was pushing his hand away. The nigga hit me. I climbed my fat ass over into the passenger side the best I could and it was on.

### *2003-September 24*

I had been feeling weird all day long. I had already lost my mucus plug a few days before today, but I was in a lot of discomfort. I started washing and going up and down the stairs just to try to move around. Then the pain started to happen every so often.

When my sister came home she started helping me take down my hair. The pain started to be unbearable at times. She was prepared for this moment. Although she was six years younger than me, she started timing the pains. We called mama who was about to be home from work and she kept saying she was not about to take me in for them to send me home. She said that the pains I was having didn't sound like contractions and they were only going to send me home. Needless to say I stuck it out and bared the pain. When she came home, she could see it in my face that at that point I was in excruciating pain.

"Come on girl! I don't have time for them to send us back home, I have to go to work in the morning. I hope they tell us something good."

We all got dressed and headed out. Mama called my whole family when we got to the hospital and told them it was time. Of course they showed up and showed out. Rocko's sister and mother even came surprisingly. He finally showed up with his brother in tow and they both had been drinking. It was embarrassing and I felt some type of way, but I was not about to allow myself to be in any distress dealing with him.

I couldn't push when it was go time, so they were threatening to do a c-section because the baby's heart rate was going down and so was mine. Once in the room preparing for the procedure, I knew shit was real, and didn't want to get cut on so when I told them I was ready to push they gave me one last time, and I did it after several tries. They had looked for his father, but he was too busy chasing behind his brother throughout the hospital. So just as I was telling them to tell my mother to come in with me he appeared. He tried to hold my hand and I declined for a minute, but I realized I needed that support, if only for a second.

I'm not going to front, that shit hurted more than any other thing I had to ever endure, but my baby was here and healthy. And that's when the game changed. Game changer – Zamir. I never in my life thought that I could ever love another human being so much until I laid eyes on him. All natural and no drugs during labor, and the welcoming of my young King. I did it! I gave birth to a human and it felt so good just to be able to hold the little person that had been occupying my body for the last nine months of my life. Just looking at him in his eyes and holding his little fingers, I knew then shit was definitely real and the game for me as I knew it would never be the same. I was ok with that because now I felt complete and felt like I had a divine purpose. Zamir was definitely the game changer in my life and I wasn't taking no shit when it came to mine!

**TO BE CONTINUED…**

## *All The Wrong Reasons*

Author: J Focuz

Sometimes in life, you're pushed to an edge that you just can't seem to back away from until it's too late. You almost feel like Wiley Coyote and that the cliff might break off as you fall into the abyss of bad intentions and ill received notions. Life was beginning to head in that direction for AJ, he just didn't have the slightest clue of how much so as of yet.

It was 4:15pm on an extremely mild Saturday for April and the only place you could find Anthony Johnson at that time was at the neighborhood dice game. It was usually comprised of low level drug dealers, scam artists, and my personal favorite, guys fresh out the bank from payday. That's sort of where AJ fit in. Notice I said sort of. He typically worked a normal 9 to 5 job, but every now and then he sold a little weed, nothing too major. He only sold enough so he could smoke for free without really any profit. So far he had been hot on the dice.

"Six plus five equals what?" said the guy in a 3M safety vest. He tossed the dice and they rolled and bumped against each other causing them to stop.

"Well I'll be got damnit," said a guy wearing jeans without a shirt as he threw his hands up. It was eleven.

"Put your money down if you wanna bet fellas, I got all night!" Anthony, the guy in the safety vest, boasted picking up one of the two twenties that lay strewn on the concrete.

So far, only 15 minutes into the game, he had won over a thousand dollars in twenties. He was completely on fire and hadn't been in months.

"Double that shit up, lil nuts," replied a voice from outside the circle they had formed. Everyone picked their heads up to see Smoke had joined in on the fun. Smoke had a southern drawl that, besides being one of the biggest dope boys in Inkster, attracted the ladies to him. Two beautiful ladies standing next to him seemed to break off into formation as he held his hand out palm up. One of the ladies took a bookbag off her back and the other reached inside and pulled out a wad of cash. The shorter and prettier of the two, in Anthony's eyes, placed the money in his hand and he counted off $3,000.

While all this was taking place, another player was coming into the game. A robbery was being prepared out back behind the project building they were shooting dice in front of.

"So look man. Ima pull up real quick, nigga just hop out with the heat," said Dirty Shawn.

"So what you mean like open the door? It's hot as two fat bitches arm wrestling inside a flat screen TV box in this car man," said his sidekick who conveniently was also named Sean.

"Man shut the fuck up man this serious brodie!" Said Dirty Shawn.

"Alright, alright man, so then what?" Sean replied.

“I hop out and shake all them niggas down. If anybody move man, just shoot em.”

“How come I always gotta be the damn shooter?”

“Cause I’m faster on my feet, man.”

Sean was a heavyweight. He barely even fit right in the car’s seats, so typically he’d sit in the back.

“So what, you think fat boy with the forty Cal. Ain’t gon’ leave em shook?”

“No, nigga it’s gone make them niggas wanna run you fat fool. Now get yo shit tight.” They had been planning this set up all month because these dice games happened only once every thirty days. They knew everybody from top level dope dealers to the working class would show up to a gig like this. Smoke was the big fish they’d been waiting for to swim into this small pond.

“Now look, while I’m shaking niggas down get they guns,” said Dirty Shawn who, of course, was the brains of the operation. It was a really simple in and out job, except for the fact 5 out of 10 men, and 2 women all had guns, of course.

“You know what, fuck dat,” said Dirty Shawn.

“Ima walk up like a shooter. Like I’m just tryna play my hand at some side bets. Sean, this the big one man, you think you can do it?” Sean was always conveniently the getaway driver and person who collected the bodies. This time, however, it seemed to be otherwise.

“On my signal man, I need you to jump out and rob everybody on the scene. How much money you got bro?”

“Money? Nigga I ain’t know you had to have money for this shit. I thought we was here to make the shit. If that was the case, I woulda came through with a knot. All I got is thirteen dollars brodie.”

“Nigga, what ima do with thirteen bucks man?” Said Dirty Shawn, annoyed yet surprisingly patient.

“Do like me bro, side bet a five till ya die, ya feel me!?” Screamed Sean as he put his hand up for a high five. Dirty Shawn stared at him while trying to keep his composure.

“Side bets, side bets” said a guy wearing a dad hat that looked like it had been washed one too many times.

“Man I got five he win on the come out,” said Dirty Shawn looking up at Anthony. Sadly, it was the working man’s turn to lose. As the side bets were being made, Anthony was swapping out his trick dice with real ones. The dice he had been shooting with were covered in two of the same number, causing him to roll seven or eleven whenever he pleased. The other two dice were normal.

“Where ya sidekick Sean at Dirty Shawn,”

shouted one of the spectators. They were always known to be together, so when one wasn't accompanied by the other, it was a weird situation.

"Alright man, let's get it," said AJ. The clamoring over whose betting who settled down and Anthony made his roll. It was a three, and that means pay taxes. He paid up his money, but was able to keep the dice and everyone with side bets placed new ones. He pulled out his trick dice again and made his roll. Being the person he is, Dirty Shawn noticed the switch. It was quick con man sleight of hand, but those were most definitely a new set of dice Anthony pulled from his jacket sleeve. That's when it struck Dirty Shawn like Solange in an elevator. He pulled out his phone to text Sean.

*Shawn – Don't pull up bro... Sent. 4:26*

*Sean – Y wassup man? Sent. 4:26*

*Shawn – He using trick dice nigga we bouta do this wit no heat. Sent.4:27*

*Sean – Den how we gon get da money? Sent. 4:30*

*Shawn – Just stay put stupid. Sent. 4:30*

After a few more wins and a "loss" by Anthony, Dirty Shawn finally had enough money to talk shit and mean it. Rather Anthony knew it or not, he had been covering for him while he swapped out his trick dice with the real ones. He had been diverting attention his way by talking trash and cracking jokes, which happened to be his specialty when money was on the line. Getting in on Anthony's trick dice con was just as good as robbing everybody for everything they had, with zero violence incorporated. That is, as long as the lil factory working asshole didn't screw up.

"Man this is borin' man these fools betting this lil petty ass money. Smoke I bet you a thousand dollars this nigga come out the gate with a seven," said Shawn pointing at AJ.

"Oh, this fool Dirty Shawn talkin cash mane now that's what I like ta hear. Small fries bounce, five hundun or better at this table," said Smoke as the small betters stood up and slightly backed out of the circle. There were six people remaining, all big time heavyweights in the neighborhood, besides AJ and Shawn of course.

There was the chicken guy's son, Amari who was seventeen. His father, Mr.Fry, owned the "You buy it, We fry it" restaurant off Inkster Road and Michigan Ave. He was sort of born into money so he always came around to feel like he was really from the streets. There was Lance, the up and coming dope man with hopes of being next in line to succeed Smoke, shall he ever need a replacement. There was also Skinz who was slightly older. Skinz had just finished his sentence up at the Ionia Prison and was the enforcer for a prostitution ring. The story was the guy had so many bodies on him he burnt down a house on Glenwood to get rid of 'em all. Then there was Anthony, Dirty Shawn, and Smoke.

"Dirty Shawn, who you hit a lick on this timbruh?" Amari asked who knew Shawn was infamous for his scams and plots to come up on a quick buck.

“Man I just been on a roll with these side bets nigga, come get some of this action.” With all eyes on Dirty Shawn, it was going to be easy for the two to clean up. What Dirty Shawn wanted to know is what put a working class guy like Anthony in a position to want to scam people who were more than willing to take his life for being screwed over?

After all bets were placed, Dirty Shawn was betting each and every person while he did his song and dance distraction. As Anthony got ready to roll the dice, he shook them up and stared at Dirty Shawn. Did this guy know what he had been up to this entire time? The bigger question was, was this guy helping him cover it all up?

For the entire game, Anthony had been rolling the dice in a circular motion, careful not to let the dice get too far away from him as he shot his point. As soon as the dice would land on their number, he would quickly swipe them up as to not let the others see the repeating numbers on the corresponding sides. It was a good plan in Anthony’s eyes, as well as Dirty Shawn’s. He had learned the trick from his father growing up poor in Inkster’s ATA area and had perfected it before he ever had to use it. Today was his first time using the technique, and probably his last.

When Dirty Shawn and Sean had pulled up in their black GMC Jimmy, they had been sure to park the car facing the action. Sean was still in the back seat of the truck with his 9 millimeter pistol inserted in the pouch on back of the passenger seat. He was still observing when he noticed Dirty Shawn look up at him. Dirty Shawn didn't just look over at him once, but several times, giving Sean a bad vibe. Sean grabbed the gun, and began to approach the gambling circle.

Anthony was hot, he had made $5,000 more than he came with and all the other players were being cleaned out like a basement in a flood. All except for Dirty Shawn.

"Ok man, I got people to do and things to see so this is my last fade," said Anthony.

"Bullshit is yo last fade. I need to make my paper back play boy," said Smoke.

He said 'boy' like 'bow' with an I at the end.

"I'll fade ya'll man I ain't trippin'!" Dirty Shawn said.

It was at that time that Anthony received a call. He picked up his money and began to walk away as he slid the green phone icon up. It was Bankroll. Bankroll was a well-known rapper in the area who got his buzz in the rap game because, well, everything he rapped about was true. He was the biggest drug dealer in Inkster and if the rumors were correct, he was on the verge of signing a major record deal. It was a call that Anthony just couldn't simply ignore. He stopped walking slightly outside the circle and spoke.

"Hey what's up bro, long time no speak?" Said Anthony.

“Yeah man, working. Slide by,” said Bankroll. He spoke in short fragments because he feared the feds would be listening in. The thing about it was, he was so used to his coded language on the phone that he spoke in fragments all the time.

“Ok bet, I’ll swing by in a bit.”

As Anthony ended the call he was forced to deal with his harsh reality. He hadn’t worked in nearly two months and he was going to lose his mother’s house. Before his mother, Linda, had passed away, she began to lose the house due to back taxes. Anthony had begun working two jobs several months ago to help her keep her home but it was never enough. Eventually, he had lost both his jobs due to the stress they had put him through trying to keep up with them. Both jobs were almost ten hours a day, lucky for Anthony one was only three days a week. It had been hard for him to keep up. After losing his mother to a brain tumor and his father being in jail, the house was his responsibility now. The four thousand dollars he had made today would pay off the taxes for the last year, but he also needed money for this year. Being out of the job he had decided to take chances.

“Look fellas, I gotta bounce,” said Anthony turning back towards the circle.

“Man, check this here out. $1500 you don’t hit on the come out,” said Smoke, eager to get a percentage of his money back fast.

“Nigga you betta take that bet,” screamed Dirty Shawn. As Sean began to approach, Anthony accepted and pulled out his trick dice for one final roll.

He shook up the dice and began to roll as the unexpected happened.

"Ha choo," Anthony sneezed as he tossed the dice. They flew from his hands and rolled directly to Smoke's feet.

"Man what the fuck!" Smoke yelled as he bent down to pick up the dice.

**TO BE CONTINUED…**

## ***Betrayal's Division and Dysfunction In The Life of Amy***

Author: A. L. Brown

This story is a condensed version of a larger story/writing. It's being told from the eyes/perspective of a nine year old girl whom I call Amy, who was unable to show emotions or express her feelings to anyone until she was in her teen years. Amy believes later that it was because of the molestation and physical abuse she endured before she was ten years old which caused deficits in all areas of her developmental stages. To this day Amy continues to struggle to find her true identity that was stolen from her during the first five years of her life.

Being in a state of confusion and unable to trust the men around Amy made her feel unsafe and unprotected by the very people that were supposed to protect her. Living in fear had become a normal way of life for Amy. The fear of being sexually or physically abused was always on her mind. Instead of running around having fun and playing with baby dolls, she was always in fear of the men that were around her. By the time Amy was ten she had begin to slip into a state of depression, which caused her to be more withdrawn from everyone. Amy always kept her feelings inside and never showed any signs of emotions. Things that were supposed to be amusing or funny to others never moved Amy.

Amy was clueless about what was going on in her little body and in her head. At that point, she didn't know how to share her feelings because she was too afraid and didn't trust anyone. When Amy was twelve her uncle tried to molest her but, she managed to break free and run to an older cousin only to have her cousin tell her not to tell anyone what had just happened to her. Unfortunately, Amy began to have behavior problems and couldn't concentrate because of racing thoughts. Amy attempted suicide by taking aspirins and was angry when she woke up in the morning so she begin cutting her wrist hoping she'd bleed to death and that would be the end of all her problems with the abusers.

Amy lived in a loveless home and never heard the words "I Love You." There was never a show of affection within the household. As a result, of the sexual and physical abuse within the first five years of her life, it affected every area throughout her developmental stages. Amy struggled with trusting people and turned to God for protection and guidance. Amy continued to struggle to find out who she really was and what her true purpose was on EARTH.

July 23, 1967, Amy's family lived on Delaware and Woodrow Wilson one block from 12th Street, which has now been renamed Rosa Parks. It was on a Sunday afternoon when Amy's mother sent her older brother Ben on 12th Street to Maxx and Karl's five and dime store to buy a pack of bobbie pins for her. Shortly, after leaving the house Ben came running back all hysterical and shaking uncontrollably.

He told her that he didn't get a chance to go into the store because he saw people fighting in the middle of the street and breaking into the stores that were closed on Sundays. 12th Street at that time was lined with clothing stores, furniture stores, TV repair shops, record shops, liquor stores, and eateries as well as places for entertainment. As a matter of fact, the Detroit Police Department had raided an after hours' club called The Blind Pig and people started fighting and it spilled out into the streets. Mostly, Jews owned businesses on 12th Street. The record shop was called The Golden Coast. It was a pretty nice size shop and was always busy. Amy's brother Ben witnessed the start of the chaos and mayhem before the looters started torching stores after breaking into them.

Amy's mother ran out on the front porch to see what she could from the porch looking down towards 12th Street. She saw people on the block running towards 12th Street. It seemed like minutes after going onto the porch, all she heard was the sound of sirens from fire trucks and police cars. 12th Street was on fire and people were running in and out of stores with an arm full of items/merchandise. As the sun began to set, the commotion and chaos intensified and fear begin to overtake Amy who's ten years old at that time. Shots begin to ring out and everyone in the house hit the floor. As the shots appeared to get closer, Amy's mother told everyone to crawl to the back of the house. Amy became frantic and began crying. Amy was afraid someone would come in and shoot and kill the whole family. They lived in a lower four family dwelling. Amy sucked her index finger and rocked back and forward when she was scared, so she begin rocking and sucking her finger and crying all at the same time. Amy's mother tried comforting her. She held her close and gently rocked her as she whispered in Amy's ear words of assurance that everything would be okay and to stop crying. Unfortunately, no one in the house slept a wink the first night of the riots. Although, there were still shots fired, it was as frequent as earlier in the evening.

The next morning we heard a loud knock on the front door. It was the landlord who lived upstairs in the same four family flat. She was telling Amy's mother that her husband's repair shop had been broken into and a lot of TV's were taken that were being repaired for customers. She also said the shop had been partially destroyed by arsonists. Amy's mother asked about the other stores on 12$^{th}$ Street and Mrs. Banks told her that all the businesses on 12$^{th}$ had been broken into and torched by looters. Although, the DPD were there they couldn't control the crowd.

By late afternoon, Amy's mother noticed a yellow taxi-cab driving slowly down our block as if he was looking for an address. She hailed him down and asked if he could take her to a grocery store in a different neighborhood. She grabbed Amy and they jumped into the backseat of the cab. Before the driver could get out of the neighborhood, snipers begin shooting at the cab and the driver's tires were hit by bullets. The driver pulled over and we all jumped out of the cab. While still being shot at, Amy's mother pushed her to the ground and laid her body on top of Amy's to keep her from getting shot by the shippers. One of the neighbors opened her door and yelled for us to run inside. Amy's mother, the cab driver, and Amy made it into the house safely. In Amy's mind she thought they were inside for hours before the shooting stopped. The tires on the cab had been flattened by bullets so the driver called for another cab to come take us home. Still didn't make it to the grocery store before being dropped back off at home.

As the sun began to set that evening, Amy's older brother JB was standing looking out the back door when he noticed a grocery basket full of food just sitting in the alley. When JB walked up to it a man asked him if he could watch it until he came back. The man walked briskly towards the direction of 12th Street. Once the man was gone JB hurried and took all the food inside and closed the back door. It had gotten dark by that time and everyone was hungry so JB popped a pizza into the oven that came out of the grocery basket. While waiting on the pizza to cook, the gun shots started up again. The National Guardsmen had arrived by now. Amy heard loud voices saying turn off all the lights and get on the floor, and then Amy heard a pop, pop, pop it was the hall lights being shot out. All you could hear in the hallway was footsteps running up the stairs to get on the roof of the building. The neighbor across the street was on his roof shooting at the National Guardsmen. It was Amy's classmate Leonard's father, the neighborhood sniper. By the time the National Guardsmen got him off his roof, the pizza had burned to a crisp. The sniper was shot by one of the guardsmen and was taken into custody. He stayed in jail until the riots were over.

Its July 25th a lil pass midnight before the guardsmen got control of the neighbor sniper. By the break of day which is Tuesday July 25th the snipers whole family, 10 kids and his wife who was a nurse at Henry Ford Hospital, were standing on the front porch. Food was no longer an issue for Amy and her family, it was all bout staying safe. The block was quiet now the sniper had been taken to jail but, people were still on 12th looting and setting fires. While Amy's mother was upstairs talking with the landlord Mrs. Banks, JB decided he would sneak out the back door and down the alley to 12th Street. Before JB could get out of sight he was spotted by Amy and her other older brother Ben. They followed JB to 12th Street.

When the three of them got to 12th there were National Guardsmen at the front and back of the stores wearing army clothes, helmets, and, long assault weapons. Amy and her brothers' walked right pass a couple guards standing in front of a store that had been broken into and looted. Amy continued to follow her brothers' as they walked over stuff all over the floor. Amy saw a single brown man's shoe that was about the length of her arm, at least she thought she'd never seen any shoe that large. Amy picked up the shoe with amazement and walked pass the guardsmen carrying the shoe. The guardsmen were letting people walk out with anything except for electronics and weapons. Amy was in big trouble when she returned home for leaving out the house with her brothers'. Amy's mother was so mad at her that she snatched the big brown man's shoe and threw it out in the backyard by the concrete garbage bin. Amy's mother had already warned her about following her brothers' around without asking her permission. It seemed to Amy that the Detroit Riots lasted longer than it really did because the nights were longer at least to Amy they were.

After, the riots were over and the National Guardsmen had left, Amy's mother took her on $12^{th}$ and it was a sight that would be embedded in her memory for the rest of her life. $12^{th}$ Street was no longer as we remembered it. Everything had been broken into and looted or burned up. Amy had dreams for a longtime after witnessing all the chaos and devastation, and being shot at by snipers.

The summer of 1968, Amy and her mother was sitting on the front porch with her lil baby sister in her stroller watching the neighborhood kids play hop scotch, tag, and enjoying the nice weather. Amy noticed a group of young guys walking down the street talking loud and making hand gestures, and a few minutes later another group of young guys were walking towards them. Both groups met up in the middle of the block, just so happen we lived in the middle of the block. They stopped in front of Amy's house. A few words were said and they were very angry about something that had transpired. They begin throwing blows at each other and the first group of young guys was called the Black Panthers. They were known by all the neighborhood peoples. Amy's mother had no idea who the other guys were. One of the Panthers pulled out a knife after being struck by another guy. The guy ended up being stabbed in the chest area and fell to the ground, his head hit really hard against the concrete. Blood was gushing up in the air coming from that guy's chest. He never moved during the whole altercation/fight.

All of a sudden, two of the guys started running towards Amy, her mother, and lil sister. Amy's mother was able to get the three of them into the house and slam the door to keep them from coming in. Amy recalled that being the bloodiest sight she'd ever seen before. Blood was everywhere, the middle of the streets, the sidewalks, and the guy's clothes were drenched in blood. The guys were bleeding through their clothes, the ones that still had shirts that is. Amy's dreams were filled with violence, chaos, physical and sexual abuse for many years.

By the time Amy was twelve she had experienced so much trauma and violence she did not know how to feel about life because she was too young to even process what she had been through. Amy had problems sleeping many nights because of reoccurring memories and had no idea at her age that she was struggling with PTSD (Post Traumatic Stress Disorder) until she reached adulthood.

TO BE CONTINUED…

## *My Little Love Story*

Author: Black Goddess Sable

### *Part 1*

I remember how I met the love of my life like it was yesterday. It was a hot, August, Fall semester day in 2012 at NMU (Northern Michigan University). I went to the Olsen Library to print out my World Religion's Syllabus and right at the print station was a very handsome white male. He had freckles, red hair, and omg his eyes were Lake Superior blue. I bee lined in front of a lot of girls to get close to him. He was talking to a very pretty white female who had goldilocks hair. I thought to myself *aww shoot, well I can't blame him for talking to her she's beautiful.*

Next thing I hear is, "excuse me can you show me how to put money on my ID so I can print out my class syllabus."

"Sure."

"Yeah the girl I was talking to before was sweet, but explained things too fast. So what's your major,

"General Biology and yours?"

"Nursing."

"Cool."

"Oh hey Dr. Belton,"

"Hi Sable, Hi Dan. I'll see you in class," Dr. Belton said.

"Wait you know Belton?"

"Yes he's my Academic Advisor."

"That's my Anatomy professor."

I was about to leave the library when i decided to walk up to Dan and stuck my hand out.

"BTW my name is Sable." He took my hand and said, "my name is Dan." He asked for my number and wrote it on his hand. As I approached my dorm I thought *this guy isn't gonna call me*. Next thing I hear is buzzzz buzzzzz buzzzzz I look at my phone and received a text message that said: Hi Sable this is Dan thank you for helping me put money on my ID and showing me how to work the print station. Oh and between you and me, I think your very pretty.

That's how we met and ever since then we fell in love.

## *Part 2*

My first year without Dan was rough. Never have I felt so alone or like an outcast. My crime involved loving an addict. People walked passed and looked at me as if I was something the cat coughed up.

"Aren't you the addict's fiancé? She used to be smart, but now she's dumb. I bet you she ran drugs with Dan. I don't feel sorry for her, she stayed with addicts. I bet she's an addict too. She got some nerve walking into church as if she's one of God's children. She deserves to be broken. God has no favor or sympathy for her."

Sable decided to have a long talk at church with her church father, Pastor Bob.

"Sable…..?"

"Oh hello Pastor Bob."

"How are you?"

"..........." All you could hear was crickets.

"I saw Dan's mom and son in church today. She told me how loyal you were to her son and glad he met you. Sable are you okay?"

"No, I feel isolated and judged by people here," Sable sobbed.

"Sable your not an addict, those who judge you don't know what you, Dan, and Julie went through. I remember Dan as a little boy."

"Wait......you knew Dan?"

"Yes, you see that church over there behind Whitman Hall?"

"Yes, Dan pointed it out to me and said he used to go there for youth group and.........Pastor Bob did you own that church?"

"Yes, I was the pastor of the church and youth group as well."

"So you knew about me and Dan?"

"Yes I know, Cliff and Eleanor told me."

"Oh Pastor Bob what you must think of me?"

"Sable we are all human, if I told you half the stuff people have confessed to me it would blow your mind. The people who come to church, a lot of them suffer with addictions such as alcohol, drugs, and sex. Yet their spouses stay with them just as you did with Dan."

"Pastor Bob, I loved Dan not the addict."

"I know, his mom told me how blessed Dan was to have you as a fiancé, and best friend. She couldn't believe a person like you existed or how much hope and love you gave him. So no Sable I don't see an ungodly woman who used drugs. I see a child of God, who used her gift of love and understanding to help a fellow child of God."

"Thank you Pastor Bob, you made my day......"

After Pastor Bob left I wept and said, "*Daniel you were never a lost cause. I believe you crossed over into the light, the addict is gone. You are free from its clutches. I believe in the signs and testimony of your family. No one is crazy, the spirit world is just as real as the human world. I believe the spirit world operates on a different plane to which we as mere mortals don't understand. I believe Daniel my blue-eyed boy, is in heaven and at peace.*"

## *Part 3*

When I came back from college I was a zombie. I didn't want to be around anyone. I spent the night in the hospital. Once I was released, I went home. My old flame Ghost texted me to see if I was at home. He came over and embraced me. The smell of Axe on his body and clothes was intoxicating. We sat on the edge of my bed and talked. He noticed my weight loss, drained energy, fatigue, depression, and my skin having a paler appearance. Ghost touched me around my neck and shoulders. It felt good to feel a man's touch again.

I started to cry and said....."Dan gave me HSV2, after he died. I started Suppressive Therapy with Antivirals. Even though the virus is suppressed, I still fear transmitting it to my partner. I promised myself that I would never give this to anyone I love and care about and..."

"Stop, you told me before and educated me about the virus, and you take the antiviral every day. Sable I know you wouldn't give me HSV2 on purpose I trust you."

My mind was filled with emotions of guilt and sexual desire. I had guilt for wanting sex with a man who wasn't Dan and I was ashamed of having sexual desires. I felt torn. Half of my mind said, “go slow, enjoy the intimacy, you deserve it, and so much more. You’ve been faithful to Dan for 2 and 1/2 years even when he spent the remainder of a year and a half in Marquette General Hospital and Marquette County Medical Care Facility. Dan knows you love him, but he wouldn't want you to deprive yourself of sex and intimacy. The other half says, “it's been 2 and 1/2 years since you had sex, your trembling, and feel dirty for having another man touch you. You always said you belong only to Dan and no one else.” I felt so scared and tired as if the weight of the world was on me.

Ghost whispered in my ear, “it’s okay.” We made love. All the pain, sorrow, depression, weakness, fear, and shame disappeared. The feelings were overwhelming. Tears formed in my eyes not of sorrow, but of hope. Ghost wrapped his arms around me and listened to my painful story.

“I’m so sorry Sable, what you must have suffered through then to have that bitch of a woman toy with your mind.” I noticed Ghost’s eyes were filled with tears.

“Ghost will you hold me?” Ghost smiled and wrapped his arms around me.

As time went on, Ghost and I became closer and closer. We haven't made it official because truthfully what's the rush, why not enjoy living in the moment. We both have gone through things in life that questioned if we want to go steady. Right now I am taking baby steps. I know ordinary people won't understand, but going slow isn't that bad. You see, I've known Ghost since high school, but at that time he was a wild stallion. He was always going after girls, but never stayed with them very long. I decided to keep Ghost to myself.

Friends would try to hook me up with some random guy and referred to my late fiance as your ex-boyfriend. They made many, thoughtless statements.

"Omg your always depressed, You know just because Dan is dead, doesn't mean your dead too. Don't you want to be happy? You have been grieving over Dan for two years, when are you going to let him go, and let another man have you? Have you forgotten all the hell and pain his addiction and bipolarism put you through? Have you forgotten the cheating and the Herpes Virus he gave you? Have you forgotten he sold your engagement ring to pay for his whore along with drugs plus rent?"

The men's comments were just as bad.

"Your trying to turn me into your ex-boyfriend. Woah, woah, woah you didn't tell me your fiance was white. So what do you hate black men? How dare you date one of us after being engaged to a white man, You have no sympathy from us. You post about Dan every day, did you ever think how a man feels when you cry and talk about your ex-boyfriend? You still have pictures of Dan on Facebook, so of course men have the right to be upset with you about it. All you seem to do is think and talk about Dan. Maybe I should pour Dan's ashes down the drain and that will make you stop thinking or speaking of him."

"SMACK! "

How dare you even think you have access to me? I regret nothing. As far as I can see and hear you are a fool. You can't erase my soulmate from me no matter how hard you try. You know nothing of love or respect. God created my soulmate and I asked for a man who loved me just as much as I loved him. I received that gift ten years later and so much more. So guess what? I decide who is worthy to have me by looking through your heart and seeing what kind of man you are? if your heart is filled with hatred, anger, racism, and, violent destruction then you are not the one for me. If that means I have to be alone, then so be it. Sometimes it's better to be alone because no one can hurt you and you get to learn more about yourself. I have been with men who were abusive - mentally, sexually, and physically. Do you really think I would go back to the slums after I had a taste of what God gave me? The old me would have, but the new me allows God to be my compass and point me in the right direction.

## *"Everywhere The Wind Blows"*

Author: Sasha

The summer of 2018 was long and hot. This particular day I was walking downtown enjoying the Riverwalk and the people all around me. It was the first day I had a chance to really take in the beauty of our city and just relax. I had just finished my thesis for college. It had taken me all summer to write something worthy for my professor. This was one of the most hardest classes I had taken thus far, but I was determined to finish my degree no matter what. I stopped to buy a smoothie at the I and a guy ran right into me. He had the most beautiful smile I had ever seen on a man. He apologized for almost knocking me over, but I really couldn't hear what he was saying, I was too busy thinking about how it will feel for him to touch me. I didn't see him again until later that day when we met. It was the most unexpected beautiful day, or that's how I was feeling anyway, up until that very moment I had been just going through life. That one touch and smile sparked something in me. Being hurt so many times before, my outlook on love was dismal. Me and my ex had been broken up over a year and I was tired of touching myself. It was only momentary pleasure, but once in a while had turned into daily doses of self-care. I longed to be held, touched, cuddled, and kissed by a man again. The day was ending so I decided to take the Q-line home for a shortcut. As I approached the boarding platform I could see the man from the I standing there. This time I wasn't going to miss my chance to talk to him. I had no idea what I was going to say, all I know is what I wanted to do. My eyes kept going back and forth from his face to his crotch. I could tell that it was a lot of man under them boxers. My vagina was pulsating so hard I thought I was going to have an orgasm right there. And then it happened, I had the ultimate orgasm like nobody's business. Here I am in public, I didn't even know that I had reached inside my skirt and inserted my fingers. It was so wet and sticky, but the sound that came out of my mouth was like a wounded animal. I was so embarrassed I played it off like I stubbed my toe.

At this point it seemed nothing could ruin my day. I licked the juices off my finger and walked over to him politely, tapped him on the shoulder, and whispered in his ear "CAN I FUCK YOU!!" He turned around and whispered in my ear ,"where?" As we boarded the train we rubbed and touched as much as we could. When we got to the last stop on the route we exited the train and he told me we could go to the St. Regis. As we walked to the hotel we finally had a real chance to talk. He told me his name was Keith and I told him my name was Sasha. It was the first time in a long time I felt a real connection to a man. I waited in the lobby as he checked us in. He told me to go to the room and wait for him, he would be back in a minute. I did as I was told, went into the room, and made myself comfortable. He was gone for quite a while so I started to wonder if he had changed his mind. Was he a murderer and I had bitten off more than I could chew? But all my fears and worries dissolved when he walked back in the room. He had the most beautiful dozen red roses and even stopped in the gift shop to buy me a sexy lace negligee. I was overwhelmed, he asked me to go take a shower, but don't dry off.

When I reentered the room he had spread some of the rose petals all over the bed. He told me to lay down on the bed. I was aiming to please so I obeyed. He stood at the end of the bed hard and erect. His skin was like looking at the midnight sky with a million stars in place. I watched as he tore open the condom pack and rolled it down his manhood. I took the biggest gulp when he kissed my inner thigh so close to my sugar bowl I thought I would explode. He gently pulled back the hood of my clit and spreaded the most gentlest kisses on a pussy any woman would kill for. I didn't even know my clit could get that big. Then I guess he wanted to test the waters so he blew on my anus. I have had some beautiful organisms in my life, but this was special. He was a magician darting his tongue from my precious jewel to my anus back and forth. I have never came so hard with a man back to back to back. When he was done feasting on me, I wanted to return the favor.

He said, "hush baby we have plenty of time for that. I want to finish exploring your body."

He turned me over on my stomach and I got on my knees. He said, "Sasha do you mind if I make you talk."

I replied "yes."

He said, "I wasn't talking to you I'm talking to my pussy." When I woke up I didn't see Keith anywhere. He didn't even leave his number, nothing. I had no way of getting in contact with him. My heart dropped, next thing I know room service was knocking at my door. He ordered me breakfast with a note saying, "enjoy the rest of the day beautiful."

Now that got me smiling really hard. Maybe it wasn't a one night stand, but I didn't want to read more into it. When I finally arrived back at my apartment I was spent. I took another shower and got dressed for my Psych class. The one thing my professor hated was anything late especially students. Seemed like the two hour class lasted eight and I still had to work tonight. It was the furthest thing from my mind. Days were starting to turn into weeks and no word from Keith. I was starting to feel ill. How could this be, though I didn't even know this man? Sleepless, night after night I would call the St. Regis hotel to see if he had left another note or anything that resembled some interest in me. Nothing seemed to be going right, but school. If I could do anything it was write essays. It had become mundane to even start my day, it really hit me at night. Why was I so obsessed with this man?

Weeks flew by and turned into months. I didn't even have the energy or will to even touch myself anymore. The last week of fall I was walking around midtown going from class to class. I was starving so I stopped by the campus food court to grab a quick bite. As I was standing in line at Culture Café, someone came up behind me and grabbed me around my waist. I turned and pushed him away and gave him my two cents, but as I looked up again I saw that it was Keith. Something in me broke, I just started sobbing and crying.

He said, "Sasha what's wrong?" I told him that I thought I was never going to see you again. The one time I had given myself to someone and I felt like we were meant to be.

Keith said, "can you please just walk with me for a moment." He didn't have to ask twice because I was already vested. I canceled my order and we walked off campus. The whole time his hand was in the small of my back rubbing up and down. This was the first time in months that my vagina cooperated. I could feel my juices dripping onto my panties. We had walked and talked so long we ended up at The Belt Loop right by the jails.

He whispered in my ear, "Sasha can I lick my pussy? I want to hear her talk." We went behind the last row of chairs on the loop and ducked into a little doorway. I picked my dress up, slid my panties over, and he went to town. I started talking.

Keith said, “Sasha let me talk to her first then we can talk again.” As soon as his hot moist breath was near my weak spot I exploded. He sucked and licked every drop of my cum off my pussy. It was like we were never apart. He quickly turned me around and entered me from behind. I screamed, “I love you!”

He said, “I love you too.”

## ***Wet Writing***

Author: Cheraee C.

Rose red was his favorite hue so Lira preordered the sexiest and skimpiest piece of lingerie she could find online. She hid it under a peacoat precisely. She had some magnified, licentious motives and planned to entice her fiancé Leven with her exterior, and then entice him with her interior. However, he wanted to endow his infatuation was fine with her.

On the rooftop of her loft building, it was a candlelight feast waiting for them. Leven only had an appetite for Lira's body and she was even more appetizing when she let her peacoat hit the ground. You could tell by the luscious smile on his smooth, chocolate face they was about to ignite some April fireworks in a New York minute.

After Leven hugged her tightly and let his hands explore her petite, chocolate curves, he stripped down to nothing, but ripped, tattooed skin. Lira's one of a kind sultry garment was ready to surrender her bare skin, but only at Leven's leisure.

Lifting Lira up in the air like a castle, he sat her down on the edge of the rooftop. It sounds scary, being so close to the edge of life, but it wasn't. Feeling outer body adrenaline rushes, as the two kissed Leven lifted up Lira's negligee and began stimulating her juicebox with a sporadic, finger rotation. She became wetter instantly because her thoughts and her desires already had her mentally wet.

"It's been 3.5 years and a month since we had sex," Leven stated.

"Technically you can't count the first time baby, it was just a test-run. My memory is a little fuzzy though; why don't you get ready to twiddle me with your fiddle,"

"I been reminiscing about this very day Lira, I just hope you do more squirting then you do running."

"I've been saving myself for you as well. Pleasure is pain so I'm gonna take every inch of you even if I gotta scream, scratch, shake, bite, squeeze, clinch, or pinch.

Leven teased Lira's clit with his joystick, and in the same instance he used his free hand to caress and fondle her breasts. Lira had never seen Leven's penis before, but now that she was feeling it swipe back and forth between her legs, she knew for a fact it was long, thick, and fat. She thought to herself,

"Damn, I can't wait to feel him deep inside of me. This is going to be by far the greatest sex I ever had, and he had too."

She rubbed his hand across his chiseled chest using her fingers to outline his packs. A second later, she threw her head back and arched her back as he entered her foreign origins. In the same motion, he took a free hand and be stroked her with finesse up, down, left, right, side to side, hard, long, deep and repeatedly as her juices leaked and seeped off of her legs and onto the concrete. He pulled her hair, he put his fingers in her mouth and let her taste her vagina as he pounded her in every dimensional position he could think of. Lira moaned and screamed so blissfully, it was too much space for her voice to echo through the noiseless air. They made love repeatedly until the both of them collapsed on the red carpet she had spread out under the table, and cuddled up with her peacoat. That was just enough heat for them for comfort with the warm, humid April breezes blowing and flowing by.

Love you baby, I wish upon a star that vision was real. Lira ended her letter drawing a kissy emoji next to her signature. She folded it two times so it would have two neat creases and stuck it into a standard sized white envelope. She wished she could seal her erotic fantasy with some red lipstick. Unless she wanted her wet letter rejected and returned, she had better stick to a lick of saliva because lipstick and perfume wasn't allowed on inmate mail.

Finally Leven was goin get his snippet of what making love to Lira would be like. Lira was a writer and Leven had read many of Lira's hit, sex scenes. Now he finally had his very own sex scene to add to his mail collection. Lira had Leven's inmate address memorized so she wrote their two addresses in cursive letters and reached in her wallet for a stamp. She peeled the stamp off and pressed it onto the corner of the envelope. Grabbing her envelope, she walked out the door and headed to the post office. In a couple of business days, Leven was going to get a reminiscent letter he would keep secured under his mattress in his cell, and read again and again until he was freed.

## ***Love Me Back***

Author: Sasha

The way the sunlight comes through your window was always brighter to me. The way the shadows fall at your doorstep was always inviting to me. Maybe cause I knew you were in there. I can feel you all over, even though your not home. The smell of your bedroom always made me kinda drowsy, kinda punch drunk. It was like slipping on a piece of you. That's where I felt the safest and was the closest thing to your touch. But I knew you were coming so I prepared for you. I pretended to be sleep when you arrived. You said, "sweetie, are you sleep?" I still didn't move, I waited for what I knew came next…The wait was too much, that first thigh kiss I almost erupted right then, but I waited for your thick, slightly pointy tongue to caress my innermost sacred place. He knew I couldn't resist his touch. But I knew he couldn't resist the way I rode him.

Up and down our bodies melding into one. Have you ever wished that a moment stood still? That's the way he always made me feel. Special, loved, wanted, desirable (his). I loved the way the light shone through his window onto my face, it always made me feel like I was home. For months and months it went this way, I felt like I had hit astride in our relationship. Things couldn't get any better so I thought.

One day I left work early cause I was feeling sick. I stopped at the drugstore near his place to get a remedy. You know how you smell something familiar in a distance, but distinctive it was his cologne. I turned around and I saw them. I felt my hands turn clammy and my knees were weak. It was my sugah and another so sweet. Flashbacks of all the times I spent nurturing our souls so one day we could be heaven sent ROLLED around in my mind. I followed them to where I knew they would be. After they entered, I waited till I thought they would be in the throws of passion and I used my key to enter. As I made my way up to my safe haven, the room where we spent countless hours daydreaming about the future, I couldn't help, but think what did I do wrong? Do I DESERVE this betrayal? I slowly turned the knob on the door and there they were. He was giving her kisses in the spot I loved so much. I just stood there fixated on the sweet gentle way he entered her stroke after stroke the way he also did me. Everything was familiar. Not once did he look up nor did she. They were melded together. He didn't LOVE me back, I thought, I was just an interlude between songs.

# POETRY

## ***"Brown Paper Suga"***

Author: Cheraee C.

I'm dark skinned and he's darker
call the darkness brown, brown skin fine
a signature on a paperback book started it
its an underground love thang
that requires a postage stamp
and a sweet letterhead
the way he writes me
it's like his fingertips are elite
they entice me with delight
his pen strokes know how to provoke me
and get me open so I daydream every day
we take turns engulfing in a
correctional confidential ballpoint play
no fancy cursive sway
the brown-skinned riddles of notoriousness
keep me, seniority is submissive
filling me up like nutrients
slick verbs of enrichment
loving him, reading him, writing him is addictive
we got a lined paper commitment
whatever type of paper he can align
I can sip on the finest wine and unwind
between the thin lines and dinner
it might seem like a sweet fairytale
but its pen winters
when nothing goes written and pen fights
raise blood pressures and fracture futures like
wounds and sutures
its bitterness in the sweetness and the waist
deepness
pauses of friction and causes of briefness
the brown sugar and paper concoction
explains the history and the chemistry…

## ***Brown Paper Suga: Part 2***

Author: Cheraee C.

I haven't found a soul
who can replenish my soul
from my soul to my soles
these incompatible soul ties
who can serenade my chocolate glow?
my brown sugar, my brown paper
I am a target by nature
I thought I found my savior
yet these saviors, thugs, and players
come in all shapes and forms
of good-looking and smooth talking
I was so incorrect and inaccurate
now I'm writing and reflecting
on all of my love chronicles
sometimes I miss my old paper
but don't tell my old paper that
it's no room in my life
for old flames, old fumes, or old tombs
I cannot become a product of my old days
or my old ways, conspiring with my old plays
sometimes my unhappiness confuses me
it makes me reminisce, second-guess, and confess
to things only my brown skin knows
I know my brown skin is unforgettable
but my subjects and syllables
have new topics and new hearts
I had to give my brown sugar a restart, a recharge
and now that I'm moving forward
I try not to veer backwards
even though I'm always tempted by my rearview
I've had some tastes and traces of chemistry
I just can't knock out of my system
some lovers just never fade

some things just aren’t resealable
some things are mental
not everything I feel is physical
sometimes my pain isn’t visible
but my brown sugar reeks love
and my brown sugar is the best
especially when you blend it with my brown paper…

## *Rehab*

Author: Don McCaskill

Everything turns me on
and I really hate it!
The decision to be celibate;
should I regret that I made it?
Can't even focus on my test.
I just wanna nut and get some rest.
But what would make me quit
one of the things I do best?
Is it the Holy Ghost
beating in my chest?
If so,
then how can I have so much love
What I know the Lord detest?

It's like I'm in rehab,
or under construction.
I'm making my flesh mad
But it's led me to destruction.
So now I'm having withdrawals
from having no draws.
I miss the smell of the action,
and the spreading of walls.
I miss the screams of satisfaction
during all those naked brawls.
All those moments of passion
and Holy name calls.

All of it was fun
but all of it was wrong.
And now the tune in my heart
sings a different song.
All of that evil done in the dark like stealth
has proven to bad for my spiritual health.

So now it's always so....HARD
and I feel so restricted.
But that's how rehab feels
when you know that you're addicted.
So I'm shutting it all down
and I'm  breaking the habit.
I'm just gonna be celibate
and let the Lord have it.

## *Apologies*

Author: Kiara Rashai

I apologize for being a pussy
yea I said it
for not telling you what I needed
I apologize for not having enough strength
I was so defeated from my own childhood
studying the surfaces
and not what's underneath
today, I surrender all burdens and struggles
I apologize for every tear
that dropped and made puddles
I was crying from past trauma, past fears, and doubts
don't get it twisted I cried mostly
from our arguments, truths, and doubts
I had this dream all planned out
cars, clothes, houses
never dreamed that my dream
wasn't a dream of ours and
our trust was as thin as blouses
I am who I am I have no shame in that
even the Libra sign and the OVO tat
I plan to don my back
I wanted so bad to have this life
I envisioned for myself
I never questioned if this is what
you really wanted for YOURSELF
I had a son that made me grow up fast
you stayed the same, you didn't have to
and I enabled that
you didn't have to worry about
doctor's appointments and babysitters
all you had to worry about is what's for dinner
my apologies for not being the woman you wanted
the kind that sexed you every day

gave it to you in every way,
and even lied to you, instead...
Instead you got this chocolate girl
who has been traumatized since birth
who knew who she was, but was engulfed in hurt
all she knew was pain from her eyelids to her toes
all she ever wanted was to live her life
on her own terms
Now apologies are in order
because here she is again
trying to fit the mold of a life that
she supposedly chose at whim
I mean sure the house, the white picket fence
the beautiful kids all looks nice
until you have to be in that house
and you don't even recognize yourself
who are you? what have you done?
you have created another life that may repeat
the cycle of people pleasing and life of tug of war
make everyone happy, forget yourself in the end
until your depression and anxiety kicks in
then your the problem...your the one
that has created all this chaos
I apologize for everything even the hurt
I promise it wasn't what I envisioned.
I apologize for being this woman
that let a man talk to me crazy
I apologize for all the times I let those words
turn physical and not leaving immediately
I apologize for all the hurtful things I have said
the times where I wished you would
find someone else instead
I apologize for thinking you would change
grow up, be the bigger person, you know have a plan
see we have a family and I just assumed
you were part of it

wanting to make the ultimate house a home
and grow old in it
I apologize for wanting more of then
what you were willing to give
I just knew I could change
what you already had revealed
as time ticks away and our seeds get older
It's hard to face those hard questions
that always seem to get bolder
kids never stay kids for long
they become adults who understand and
no longer can hear the same tired ass song
they see everything and hear EVERYTHING
I apologize for allowing them to see those parts
that was too sensitive to their mind frames
It's so easy to point the finger, yes I know
I know for me this was not easy
pointing the finger at yourself and so
I apologize for being this complicated woman
who wanted more from a man than
what she was willing to fulfill for herself
who pointed the finger at the man in the beginning
but now had to look at herself
I apologize for being this enabler
I apologize for not being honest
there were times where I didn't want to do nothing
but I put my head down and thundered thorough it
I apologize for not taking care of myself
I chose to take care of you and your feelings
I neglected myself
I was a lousy housewife, really didn't clean
after being disrespected so many times
I gave up on a couple of things
never really said anything just let time go by
now I'm sitting here wondering
how we got this far

a fire is burned in me
however, I will not quit
Whether we make it or not
I tried with all my might
and that's something truly legit
two months til I turn 30, I expect it to be lit
hopefully it doesn't involve apologies to myself
as I cry in silence and sit.
who is this that I apologize... myself
for not being true to the word goodbye, shit.....

## ***Lock Eyes***

Author: Don McCaskill

Locking eyes
come alive.

They wander
back and forth,
side to side
from your beautiful eyes
to your switching hips
and rolling thighs.
Just a glimpse
And I have to grip
myself
as I roll my eyes
back up to catch your bottom lip
wrestling with your teeth
'till u let it slip.
Perfect timing
as I see your eyes come up
From just below my hip.

I peep your line of sight.
I see the fire
through the windows of your soul.
I'll extend my hose for the firefight.
I just may fire in the hole.
Fighting fire with fire.
Fighting passion with desire.
Add a match and kerosene
and just like an action scene
We can be explosive
And make a climax higher
higher than you've ever seen.

The moment I saw you we both froze.
What lies behind those eyes?
Lord knows.
It was him I impulsively called
when I saw your face.
Trying to control the thoughts
That race in my mental space
of you riding my face in a dark place
to your own pace.
Nonstop till I know
all your lips' cries.
This is what I feel
Whenever we lock eyes.

## ***Something About The Streets***

Author: Cheraee C.

these roads, highways, and byways are your favorite
you spend valuable time in these
cities, hoods, and old neck of the woods
time that you should be spending
with me, your, my, and our kids
you always gotta go somewhere
your always gone somewhere
steady moving from place to place
like green light traffic
why can't you ever just chill and be still with me?
you never want to be at home sweet home
until your fleeing and running
from a new principality, a new conscience,
a new reality
you only come to home sweet home
when your done playing single, devil's advocate, or
the addict lead, trophy, award-winning roles you play
your nobody's driver
except for mine
you don't have a chauffeurs' license or CDL's
you don't need to be behind nobody's wheels
none of the Big Three automobiles
your nobody's rider
except for mine
let people ride and stride
into their own crossfire by their lonesome
don't let their free will ruin your free will
I'm sure it's a street with my name on it
in somebody's state
but my components aren't made out of
concrete, asphalt, brick, or cobblestone
I'm a pure, natural woman
and I give all the sweet, concrete, unconditional love

you need
yet you behave like a little hoodlum
you behave like a little roadrunner
why didn't you marry the streets then?
I told you I wasn't sharing you
with nobody or nothing
and I meant every word that I said
it's nothing in the streets for you, me, or nobody
but if that's where you wanna be
so be it
because the streets ain't got nothing on me
I don't care what street you go on
it's gonna be your loss, your fault,
and your gonna be big mad
when you finally accept your destiny
I'll be long gone…

## *Love - in My Mind*

Author: Don McCaskill

I see you,
but I can't make you out...
who are you??
what is this about?
you get closer, coming into view with clout.
this is that idea of love
no doubt.

I love this nightmare.
I hate this dream.
your constantly convincing me
to make you a real thing.
using inception
to control my perception
of how love is "supposed" to go.
but it's really deception
because you can't have discretion
about things you don't know.

and although you come close to me
I can't find you in any place.
although your in all my dreams,
I still can't see your face!
I can't make out your figure
I can't see your shape
I can only see us from your eyes
like I'm watching a tape.

you show me us, and all of our potential
you've showed me enough
to get locked in my mental.
Its like we've been dating forever;
you've been my comfort for some time..

you make me feel better
and guilty at the same time

I feel guilty when I see you.
like I'm cheating on reality
when I visit you in my mind,
my real girl a get mad at me
getting you two to agree
has been a real issue of mine.
because I always start a problem
when y'all two misalign

nonetheless
we have gotten married and had kids
we've been on vacation of every kind.
we laugh and talk over wine to unwind.
every time I come home is like the first time we met.
your smiling eyes get so big
never filled with disdain or regret.
romantic dinners, sometimes candle lit
as I smile and share food with a silhouette
I messed around and had a whole relationship
with all the concepts I love,
and all the things I expect.

and I have all these visuals
of what love is "supposed" to be
but the truth is that it just isn't reality
see, we all picture love so beautifully
and we view it like they show us on TV.
but love isn't at all like Disney.
things don't always work out so quickly

I've learned these lessons through my mental infidelity
I've blocked my blessings
trying to make you a reality.

in fear that if I don’t then I may have to "settle"
instead of accepting the beauty of real love,
without the need to meddle.

I'll never find real love
with you in the back of mind
I'll never find a comparison
because you are my design.
God surely made something better
and his methods are divine
but I could never marry her
until I divorce the woman in my mind…

## ***No More Chances***

Author: Cheraee C.

I've risked a lot of champion chances
love may be unconditional
but all these chances are becoming unconventional
I've given you so much
more than any human being
has ever given me
more then I've given any of my
short run romances
more than any woman before or after me
will ever give you
the tolls have been high
through the love I've given
your non-deserving of such luxurious love
all you had to do was hold me down
love me back, love me right
but now I see
you can't even hold down a nail with a hammer for me
this is our second time falling in love
just how deep is a second chance?
you ain't head over heels for me
if you ain't candlelight me, dozen roses me, getaway me
upgrade me yet?
you've been breezing and sleazing by
burying us in the hardest times
I've given you too many chances for
states and dates of discomfort and regret
I can't waste another chance on you
I don't have it in me
your well has run dry
I believe in you
but I can longer believe in our love
so I give up
please let me go
don't one more chance me
don't say this time will be different
because it won't be

it's too late, your too late
your stuck in love with your ways
and I've made up my mind
I'm not giving you no more chances
I told you last time was the last time…

## ***Someone Different***

Author: Don McCaskill

A different woman in bed every night.
I thought this is what I wanted
I thought this is what I liked
it always looked so appealing
rolling around, butt naked
love swinging from the ceiling.
with someone different every night.
like it was going outta style.
I figured it was cool,
I'd do it for a while.

laying in my bed
a different person every night
my heart goes dead
once I turn out the lights.
I don't care about your problems
I don't care about your life.
I just wanna get this over with
end it all tonight.

here we go again
a different woman in bed
I was suppose to study tonight
but I'm giving some head instead.
it was a light skinned girl yesterday
and Spanish the day before
now it's dark chocolate
I'm a whore for more.

I used to preach about one,
now I brag about many.
I had one worth a hundred,
now, 100 worth a penny

so what's it all worth?
my soul stays in plight
someone different in my bed
it was me......every night.

## ***Sunset Dreams (erotica)***

Author: Sasha

The sunset felt so right,
the sun was still aglow
resting it's eyes on my body just right.
The wind was a little warm as it set me afire
blazing warm trails down my neck.
The way it kissed my skin was all consuming,
it was toying with my sensuality.
But does it know the way it makes me feel?
All tingly in my belly, yeah it does.
Does it know every touch makes me moist?
Does it know that my flesh is yearning for him to put
out the fire that is raging out of control almost
reaching my soul?
That one strong vein pulsating in my hand,
I almost sucked it.
I spread my generous thighs and turned my head
slightly to see it was my own fingers entering me.
Damn!!

## ***Enslaved***

Author: Don McCaskill

I want compensation,
reparations for my time.
I was enslaved to you.
Your love kept me bound.
You took me from the field
and into the house.
From picking the field,
to picking the drapes.
From whips and chains,
to a ball and chain.
So enslaved to you.

I want compensation.
Reparations for my time.
40 acres and a kid?
A picket fence and a dog?
I felt like three fifths a man.
Only getting partial rations,
table scraps of your energy.
Yet you benefit from the fruit of my labor.

I want compensation.
Your profit was the image of perfection.
A career, matrimony, and a family.
But my ideal image was irrelevant.
Because I was taken from my home.
My soul sold to you at a price,
my life, enslaved to you.

But I'm free now.
I ran-away,
when you weren't paying attention.
Which conveniently, was most of the time.

I was always enticed by the taste of freedom.
By the look of freedom.
Or just maybe a new massuh
who won't leave me in heat for so long.
Whose land appeared to be
a little easier on the eyes,
a lot more fun to till,
and far more beneficial for all parties.
Which leads me to question,
is freedom what I really want?
Nah, I just want compensation,
a return on my investment,
and reparations for my time.

Made in USA - Kendallville, IN
1188916_9781513648767
02.19.2021 1603